Tales Galore:

And A Whole Lot More

Copyright © 2013 Skipper Duncan

ISBN: 061581560X
ISBN-13: 9780615815602

All rights reserved.

Contents

Introduction vii

Toad Tucker Tales 12
- Fine Wine and Cowboys 12
- Weddings and Briskets 18
- The Perfect Whiskey 26

Stories Collected from Rodeo Friends 29
- Trappers 29
- Bear Attack 36
- Everything Just Went Blank 42
- Billy Hogan 44
- Fist Fights 51

West Texas Lingo 57
- Max Tankersley 57
- Bill Shaw – Linguist 62
- Accents 64

Win a Few 67
- The Big Sting 67
- The Waiter and the Water in Albuquerque 74
- Reunion Story 78

Lose a Few 81
- Rob Junell 81
- Blake Duncan – Young Farmer 86

SOME GET RAINED OUT.. 91

DO-OVERS... 97
    A DALMATIAN ON THE BED 98
    HANDSOME LES AND CAROL SANTRY 100
    BOY'S TOWN TOUR 101
    SUMMARY: DO-OVERS 106

CLASSIC INSULTS 110
    THE FAST CALF 112
    THE NOT-SO-BIG BUCK 112
    FEW WORDS BUT GREAT WISDOM 114
    NOT EXACTLY CRAZY, BUT – 115
    YOU GOTTA HURRY 116
    THE SPEEDING TICKET 119
    TWO-WAY RADIOS 121
    THE HARLEY-DAVIDSON MAN 123
    THE PERSONAL TRAINER 125

DYNAMITE STORIES... 127
    TOMMY NASWORTHY 128
    THE CESSPOOL 130
    RATTLESNAKES AND DYNAMITE 132

RUNNING STORIES.. 136
    ALLEN HAMBLEN – RUNNER 136
    CHARLIE BOB STRYKER, NON-RUNNER 139

HORSE TRADING... 142
    A BRIEF LOOK AT THE RULES 142
    COON HOUND CHARACTERS 146
    THE MINNEAPOLIS-MOLINE TRACTOR 150
    THE OFFER 151

The Chevrolet Suburban	153
Roping Horses	155
The Hippie's Horse	160
Terry Ford	163
The Horse Trade	166

Tales Galore ... 171

Chain Saws	171
Great Advice	174
The Irrigation Pump	176
Prude Ranch	178
6666 Country	180
The Perfect Arrowhead	183

Poetry ... 189

Pranksters ... 203

Tommy Buckner	204
Bob Hamblen	212

Thanks ... 221

Biography ... 225

INTRODUCTION

This book is supposed to be funny. Or at least I hope readers will find it to be so.

My collection of true tales touches on a variety of topics. Almost always, the stories are fairly short, but they finally arrive at a punch line of some kind that, at the time it happened, tickled my funny bone and burned itself into my memory bank.

Who knows what causes your gray matter to file away some event in your cranial archives? Big events almost always find a place somewhere – your wedding(s), the birth of your children, contests won or lost, dangerous encounters, sage advice from a parent or mentor, or maybe those "ah-ha" insights when you first grasped some important truth. Humorous experiences will sometimes make the cut, too. At least they have for me.

Importantly, humor seems to be an effective antidote for many ailments. No matter how tense things get, a bit of humor always seems to help.

Hilarious events sometimes come and go before you can even push the "record" button on your memory panel.

Tales Galore: And a Whole Lot More

Other times, a gifted storyteller might weave a tale which finally leads you to the side-splitting finale. With the rush of modern life, lingering conversations are almost an endangered species. Television, of course, started the trend many decades ago. It wasn't long ago that friends began to swap news, stories and jokes via a computer. Nowadays, there are even faster, more abbreviated forms of communication via iPhones. How many times recently have you noticed a group of people in a restaurant diddling with their phones instead of talking to each other?

Speaking of television and the professional comedians you see: Much of their humor is the machine gun kind. One-liners galore. Rodney Dangerfield was a master of this genre, but there have been countless others from Red Skelton to Bob Hope. I'm showing my age here and that's OK. The humor in the pages to follow comes in a different, slower form.

Even since I started hosting hunters for guided and outfitted hunts back in the mid-1980s, the epicenter of the operation seems to be our outdoor fire pit, pictured on the cover of this book. Weather permitting, hunters and guides will gravitate to that sacred spot. It is there that old-fashioned conversations flourish. One thing for sure, you are not subjected to commercial breaks every five minutes.

That fire pit, built by Pedro Contreras, the same craftsman who constructed the original adobe structure which ultimately evolved into the "Adobe Lodge," is not complicated or fancy. Pedro, being a master "albanil" or stonemason, stood fire bricks on their ends in a circle maybe 6 feet in diameter around the dirt floor of the pit. He positioned limestone rocks around the perimeter and mortared everything into place. As it turned out, that size just happened to be perfect to germinate conversations. Tons of wood have been burned there over the years.

Introduction

Yes, yes, you want to be on the upwind side, especially if your lungs are vulnerable to smoke. And on those days when there is virtually no wind, the smoke will drift 360 degrees causing periodic relocation of the participants in the pow-wow.

But for some mystical reason, that environment spawns conversation. Quality, of course, varies. Some dialog is instantly forgettable. So be it. Other times, the topics are sufficiently spellbinding that more logs are heaved onto the coals to keep the magic moment alive. It has been my good fortune to hear many classic yarns in that environment, and some of them are included in this book.

I like to remember the funny ones. To be sure, I do enjoy stories of dangerous events, business deals that failed or succeeded, wild animal tales from Africa, horse-wrecks from my cowboy friends, political discussions, or problem-solving tips on a variety of topics. But the humorous stuff somehow gets a higher priority in my memory bank.

Not all of the material in this book was learned around that fabled campfire, of course. But it came from similar situations that happened somewhere, sometime. As I stated earlier, humor seems to be more easily remembered than disasters. But something has to trigger the memory for it to be recalled. Over the past couple of years while working on my book-writing projects, I have carried a pocketful of cards to quickly jot down some long-forgotten yarn which suddenly appeared from nowhere.

Now to tell the types of stories included in this book, I have to "set the scene," so to speak, since many readers of these yarns will be unfamiliar with the subject matter. If I wrote only for the rodeo and roping crowd, or for hunters, or for ranchers and farmers, much of the background material could be eliminated, or dealt with in a couple of sentences. But who knows who will wind up with a copy of this epistle?

To finally arrive at climax of the anecdote, I have to be sure that the surprise ending will be understood and effective. Inevitably, this format sometimes necessitates a look at history. For example, we haven't always had cell phones. And there was a time when honest-to-goodness ranching-for-profit dominated West Texas. There hasn't always been so much of the recreational use of land we see today. So sometimes, taking a look back is the only way to do justice to a story. If you just happen to learn a smidgen of history in these pages, count that as a plus.

I always liked to read the O. Henry books or the mystery tales told by Sir Arthur Conan Doyle in his series on Sherlock Holmes. The twist in the story at the end of the tale made them famous. But one thing for sure – both of these legendary authors give us a great look at the times in which the stories occurred. They are filled with practical history – modes of transportation and communication employed back then to name just two. Maybe this book will have that same effect for young readers who don't remember the days of yore.

In those great authors' books, each chapter is easily managed in one sitting. Once you arrive at the climax, you finally understand how all the background information was important to the culmination of the prose. The stories in this book follow that pattern not because I am trying to compete with either of those gifted writers but simply because that format is the best way of leading the reader to the point I want to emphasize.

And that point is supposed to be funny. Maybe it wasn't so funny at the time it happened, especially if I happened to be the butt of the joke, but "in the fullness of time," upon reflection, the humor was genuine and memorable.

In putting together material for my earlier book, "Characters and Critters," I learned somewhere that a book needs a "theme." So that initial effort chronicles my

INTRODUCTION

transition from rancher to outfitter, and I included many of the humorous events which happened along the way.

But does a book devoted to humor really need a theme? Maybe. Maybe not.

As far as I can tell, only the chapters in this book seem to have a loose connection of some kind. Within each section, the subject matter is likely to go any which-a-way. The overall book, however, has no common thread other than humor. Every piece builds the scene to finally arrive at a line which, hopefully, will bring a chuckle. Or maybe even a belly laugh or two. For whatever reason, the stories included here didn't make the first book, not because they weren't funny, but because they didn't quite fit the outline of the earlier book.

Many, many readers of my other book encouraged me to write another. I can't be sure, of course, but I think I saved the best for last. So, here 'tis.

TOAD TUCKER TALES

FINE WINE AND COWBOYS

During the modern era, you can take a cowboy out of his natural element and place him in any number of fancy settings. But you'll have heck subduing his congenital penchant for pranks.

Toad Tucker, reared in the cowboy country of the Brazos bottoms near Waco, was an ordinary cowboy for years. It finally dawned on him that a future in that lifestyle would provide few comforts and zero security. After his college days at Texas A&M, he found a rewarding career selling animal health products for a huge agri-business pharmaceutical company. Ultimately, he finally became their sales manager.

On his rare days off, Toad enjoyed helping ranchers work their cattle, but such opportunities were infrequent. Toad spent most of his time,

TOAD TUCKER

not on horseback, but riding an airplane to yet one more meeting, convention or sales event for his company.

Many of the executives in agri-business have backgrounds similar to Toad's. Yes, for sure, their roots might be in the country and almost all of them are more comfortable in boots and jeans, but wisdom guided their career choices. Instead of drawing dayworker wages on some ranch somewhere, the converted cowboys positioned themselves to earn handsome salaries, bonuses and stock options for their services to the huge corporations. Similar to the days of old, they "ride for the brand" representing the interests of their various employers. Not every one of the neck-tie-wearing troops in agriculture fits this description, of course, but an impressive number of them are cowboys at heart and will always be classified as such.

To illustrate this point, Toad told the following story years ago and I thought it was a good one.

Toad and a colleague, Sam, were on an important business trip to Chicago. As employees, they were privileged to enjoy one of the perks of that lifestyle – an expense account. Plans were made to eat at a fancy place in Des Plaines – a suburb on the northwest side of the city. "Café la Cave," a rather pricy French place, didn't seem to fit the style of the two cowboys, but they had both heard all about its Chateaubriand. Cowhands do like their meat.

Once seated in the elegant surroundings, and as their eyes adjusted to the dim lighting, they spotted a friend, another agri-businessman, being seated at a nearby table. He seemed to be all alone. Greetings and nods were exchanged. When it became clear that Jack was expecting no one, Toad and Sam insisted he join their table. Jack was delighted to do so and immediately accepted their offer.

Just like Toad and Sam, Jack had been a sho-nuff cowboy in his younger days. But looking at him now, you'd never know it. In fact, he could have been mistaken for a French diplomat. Elegant, he was, standing ramrod straight in perfect business attire possessing impeccable manners. The metamorphosis, at least as far as appearances went, was flawless. To express his thanks for their kind invitation, Jack insisted on buying a somewhat expensive bottle of wine for the group. He made an appropriate head signal to the alert sommelier. The chief employee was standing at a discreet distance, hoping to be called to action by this notable group of men. He was.

Approaching the table respectfully, the wine steward quickly produced an impressive, leather-bound list detailing their substantial inventory of wines. Being an incurable wine snob, Jack loved every element of this game that was now under way. He had years of experience and knowledge of the intricate traditions of the process. In fact, Jack probably knew more about wine than the snooty wine steward. Toad and Sam, the other two cowboys at the table, sat there watching the show. They had no idea what was coming, but they both knew it would be good.

With a practiced style, Jack carefully studied the wine list as the steward stood by helpfully to offer suggestions if any were needed. None were. Finally, after an inordinate amount of time, Jack found a wine, improbably named "Cakebread," that met his exacting standards. Jack characteristically insisted on a particular year and the competent steward assured him that vintage date was, indeed, available.

The wine steward offered his obligatory praise for Jack's selection. Jack beamed, knowing that his practiced style had been duly noted. But the sommelier had no doubt who was the better man when it came to wine and all its trappings. He had dealt with highbrow behavior many times and loved the challenge.

Toad and Sam were keeping score and realized they were witnessing a world-class competition between a conniving wine elitist and a pretentious wine steward. All this would be as exciting as the matched calf roping each fall at San Angelo. To the two spectators, it was not yet clear who was ahead – the condescending SERVER or the cosmopolitan SERVED. The skirmish would continue momentarily, and if bets could have been placed, both would have taken their buddy, Jack, without hesitation.

Until the wine arrived, the three cowboys talked business. With Jack working for a different company, industry gossip dominated the conversation. This game was more subdued than the pending wine saga. With others in your field, you probe for useful information revealing as little as possible about your own inside secrets. All three were old hands at this corporate dance.

Business on that particular night in the elegant restaurant was a bit slow. As a result, and luckily, the cowboys were the beneficiaries of extra attention from the staff. The sommelier stood by as one of his troops brought in a bottle-chilling device while another fetched a container of ice. A third employee was holding the now-arrived bottle of wine as if it were a newborn child. He had a perfect, white napkin draped over his left arm. Deftly, he tipped the label over that protected arm in Jack's direction for the obligatory inspection and approval.

A miniscule nod from Jack moved the process to the next critical step.

Yet another employee in a perfectly-starched uniform suddenly appeared from nowhere. His role was to actually open the famed bottle. With several proficient twists of his wrist to the stainless steel device which hung from a chain around his neck, the waiter had the cork where he wanted it – outside the bottle. He quickly twirled it free from the corkscrew and reached for a small dish which had been placed unobtrusively for this very purpose by one of the other hands. Toad and Sam watched in rapt attention, not wanting to miss anything.

The waiter, extending the small plate now holding the cork to Jack, knew that this ritual had suddenly become the entire center of attention, not only to each of the diners but also to the numerous staff standing in rapt attention nearby. Jack, using his left hand, carefully took the cork between his thumb and forefinger. Raising it to his nose, he gave it a moderate sniff and a worthy examination keeping his eye peeled for any flaw in that stopper. So far, so good. Everything was unfolding as faithfully and traditionally as the Star-Spangled Banner played at the rodeos back home, Toad thought.

Then, ever so subtly, Jack produced a faint alteration in the ritual. Toad and Sam had known it was coming – they just didn't know when. Or what might unfold. But they knew Jack, and despite his elegant appearance and manners, they knew he was pure-dee country just as they were. Something huge was about to happen. They could sense it as clearly as they could tell when a horse was on the verge of pitching.

Still holding the cork in his left hand between his forefinger and his thumb, Jack reached for a nearby butter knife. The efficient waiters had already brought a basket of rolls earlier, together with a dish of butter. Jack scooped up a generous amount on the point of his new tool and smeared a good dollop of the stuff right on top of that cork.

The wine staffers in attendance gave a quick, horrified glance toward the sommelier, their impeccable leader. They were anxious for instructions on how to deal with this unconventional breach of etiquette. Until now, the sommelier had frankly been a bit bored with the process. Suddenly, alarm bells (figuratively) were going off everywhere. He was watching the guest paint butter on that wine cork. His eyes could not lie to him. Every staff member stared transfixed.

No one knew what to do except just stand there and hope for the best.

Sensing now that he had everyone's attention, Jack took his time. He molded that butter around that cork as if he were creating a sculpture of some kind. He must have spent a full minute on the creation. No one had said a word. How could they? They were all thunderstruck. Except for Sam and Toad, who were biting holes in their lips to keep from spoiling Jack's scheme. The wine steward had quickly arrived at Jack's side, but he dared not say anything, mainly because he had neither experience nor words to employ for what he was watching. This was a first.

Jack had spotted the arrival of the head man just off his right side, but he avoided eye contact as he planned his next move. Returning the knife to the plate, Jack easily lifted the perfectly-buttered cork to his lips. Quickly now, he bit off about half of the thing and began to chew carefully, looking absently across the room as if in deep thought. Each staff member was guilty of staring open-mouthed at the spectacle that was unfolding before their very eyes.

After an unbearably long silence, (it takes a while to chew up half of a cork, even if it has been generously slathered with butter), Jack swallowed his meal. He let things settle momentarily in his stomach as he patted his lips with his huge white napkin.

Pensively now, Jack finally glanced at the astonished sommelier. With a world-weary tone in his voice, he declared solemnly:

"It's a good cork. But it's not a great cork."

Toad and Sam could hold their guffaws no more. Had they already been drinking that wine, it would have sprayed out their noses.

The wait staff, too, quickly realized that a giant, huge trick had been played on them. They all doubled-over in laughter.

The sommelier, equally tickled, shooed his hysterical troops to a side room so as not to disrupt the other diners. Had the perpetrators been wearing their boots and jeans, he might have expected such hijinks. But certainly not from what apparently had been high-rolling businessmen.

Come to think of it, cowboys should somehow be branded so you can be alert for their pranks. Which are as sure to come as day follows dawn.

Weddings and Briskets

When young couples decide to get married, their parents and relatives, plus the friends of their parents, provide an incredible amount of support for the pending event. The enormity of this backing will not dawn on the lucky betrothed until a couple of decades later when it comes their turn to bless the marriages of their children and their friends' offspring.

In our culture today, the new couple usually enjoys a bonanza of parties and gifts. But if you were to record all the benefits in a "life's ledger," you would surely spend more on future gift commitments than you received back during your big event. The same phenomenon is true with graduation gifts. Your present jackpot will be entirely outpaced by future obligations, but that fact is not on your radar screen. Even if you did know what your unprofitable future might hold, how could you get out of the trade anyway?

But that's OK. It is somehow inappropriate to keep track of debits and credits regarding giving or gifting. Benevolence is supposed to come from the heart. Just remember to send those "thank-you" notes.

When young couples get engaged, a complicated campaign unfolds. Mothers, aunts, and grandmothers jockey for leadership roles in the operation. Dates are set; reservations are made; events are scheduled. Females compete for decision-making privileges. Truthfully, each gal wants to run the show. Males play only minor supporting roles since their interests and ideas are not worthy of consideration by the command staff.

Once upon a time years ago, there was a situation right here in San Angelo where men were actually able to participate in an event associated with a wedding. With males involved, as you might imagine, the affair almost turned into a disaster. Here is what happened:

Dale and Kay Bates, parents of the groom, Devin, were and still are super-close friends of Steve and Pollyanna Stephens, the parents of the bride, Liz. If you are still with me, you will quickly conclude that the children of friends were getting married. That is exactly the way it was. Devin and Liz had grown up together and probably didn't even remember when they had not known each other. Now each family was furnishing a child for the upcoming wedding.

Now don't let all this get too complicated. Both the Bates and the Stephens families were friends with the Hamblen and Duncan families. The Hamblen's and the Duncan's were going to provide an event to bless the coming union. As mentioned earlier, this is where the males would have an important role.

I don't remember the exact genesis of the plan, but when Devin and Liz were set to be married, Bob Hamblen and I hosted a "tool party" for Devin. If women have showers where they are gifted with all the "stuff" it takes to run a household, a similar party for the groom would be a good idea to provide him with plenty of tools that are sure to come in handy as his new wife puts him to work around the homestead hanging curtains and building dog houses.

So a date was set for the big shindig. A "Tool Party" was planned for late March. It was to be a noon-time gathering. The river park down by the dam on the Duncan Ranch seemed to be a good venue for the men-only affair. In looking at that early spring date, you can almost always count on pleasant weather in West Texas. Nope, the leaves would not yet be on the trees. But during that time of year, temperatures are quite pleasant and shade isn't at the premium it will be a few months later.

If the guests were to bring gifts of tools for the groom, Dr. Hamblen and I would be obliged to furnish them with a credible meal of some kind. The most traditional dish served in West Texas is barbecued brisket, beans and potato salad. Such fare is almost always appropriate for any gathering. For the all-male group of 50 or so, mesquite-flavored brisket was the easy choice, especially for this very good reason: I already had in my possession sufficient briskets – cooked, wrapped and frozen – left over from the previous hunting season.

Briskets, if skillfully cooked, are most enjoyable. Weighing from six to 12 pounds, the big hunk of meat is a challenge to prepare correctly. The process cannot be hurried or you'll have briskets burned on the outside and raw on the inside. Slow cooking is the secret. Using mesquite coals, chefs are ever-alert as they endeavor to keep the temperature in their oven within the correct range. Overcooked briskets dry out and have no flavor. Properly cooked briskets are moist and delicious, easily kept for future use. Just wrap and freeze them. They will be good for months if everything is in order.

I just happened to have six briskets left over from the previous hunting season. If nothing else, they would be ready for use during the coming spring turkey season. I had wrapped and frozen the briskets myself and remembered it quite well. It was the last day of the season. Hunters were leaving, the staff was departing, and I was inundated with all kinds of wind-up duties. The briskets, having been cooked overnight, were still quite warm as I readied them for the freezer. Luckily they had already been wrapped in foil for the final stage of the cooking. Using our good butcher paper in the skinning shed and plenty of tape, I put further paper layers on each brisket to prevent any freezer burn before placing the treasures into one of our big freezers. All that was done back in early January.

Now it was late March. The party was scheduled to commence at noon on a Saturday. I had thawed out the briskets the day before and only needed to heat them in the oven inside the lodge while cooking a pot of beans on the top of that stove. Expert chefs had told me that briskets of that size would feed about 10 men. With six briskets, I should be well-supplied for the group of 50 guests at the tool party. Co-host Bob Hamblen was bringing the salad and drinks. He had also acquired all the condiments, paper plates, cups, etc. No doubt his beautiful wife, Cybee, had done most of the chores. Bob is no more of a cook than I am, but he is a willing worker. The river park was ready to go and a grand event was about to get under way.

Indeed, the guest list included some of the most prominent names from the San Angelo social register. Both the Bates and the Stephens families were quite well known and moved in elite circles. The groom's dad, Dale Bates, had been a banker at the town's largest, most prestigious institution. He was on a first-name basis with every big-shot in the Concho Valley. Steve Stephens, the father of the bride, was our town's most successful businessman. He was the founder and CEO of a corporation which owned and managed scores of convenience stores with hundreds of employees. Both fathers knew oodles of important men in our town. Moreover, since both families attended the First Presbyterian Church, many prominent elders and deacons from that congregation were to attend, as well.

There had never been such a gathering of local luminaries at my ranch. I wasn't totally intimidated, but I was mildly apprehensive. No, I'm lying. I was scared to death. This was to be one hell of a huge deal. Local celebrities would be knee-deep down at my river park, all walking around with mental clipboards to record their impressions of the venue and their host.

I had been up since 5 a.m. getting everything on my end ready to go. I had heated the briskets in the kitchen stove at the lodge. It was going to be much easier working from there. Once properly heated, the briskets could be sliced and served out of the large stainless steel pans from our well-stocked pantry. They would remain plenty hot until the noon meal.

Bob Hamblen was already down at the river getting things organized. He would greet the arriving guests and set up a place where the gifts could be accumulated. Bob, being an accomplished extrovert, was the perfect "maiter-dee" for the affair. Everyone loves Dr. Bob.

It was about 10:30 that morning when I began carving the briskets. I removed the first one and did a credible job with the sharp knife I had found. Not bad at all. Of course, as any cook will do, I just had to sample a small piece. Quality control, you understand.

Now it was time for the second brisket. I was right on time. I sliced that dude up just like an expert and once again sampled a little sliver just for the heck of it. But what's this? That piece tasted mighty peculiar. So I tried another bite from a different place on the brisket. Same awful taste. Same sorry story. Hmmmmm...what could be wrong here? Sure as heck, this portion of meat was not fit to eat. Why, I don't know. It would have to be discarded. Hopefully, the five remaining briskets would still be plenty for the assembled, distinguished guests. I'll get to the bottom of the mystery later. There were still four more briskets to cut up. And the clock, she was a-ticking.

Tragically, the next brisket was as bad as the second had been. So was the fourth – and the fifth – and the sixth, the last of the inventory. Out of the six briskets, only one of them had been found fit to eat. Their offensive flavor would be impossible to disguise with any kind of sauce or seasoning. The taste reminded me of rotten cardboard. I thought I was sucking on an old dishrag used to clean lawn furniture.

Now, it was well past 11 o'clock. Out the open front door of the lodge, I could see some early traffic headed toward the river park. I had only one useable brisket. And all the well-known guests were probably already on their way out from town. It was a 20- to 30-minute trip, depending on your departure point. Jesus fed a mighty crowd with only a few fish. I couldn't imagine how Bob and I were going to feed 50 hungry men with only one brisket, a pot of beans and some potato salad.

Then, surprisingly, the phone in the lodge rang. It was Toad Tucker. A miracle was about to unfold.

Toad had been invited to the party. As he was leaving his house in town, he called on his cell phone just to check in. Graciously, he asked if he might bring anything I had forgotten. You talk about a phone call from heaven. I offered up a silent prayer on the spot.

Quickly, I told Toad about my dilemma. I needed some briskets, and I needed them now. Go to that barbecue place over on the Bryant Thruway, I told Toad, and buy me five briskets. Bless his heart. Toad immediately grasped the severity of the crisis. He had reversed course and was on his way to procure the meat even before we bid goodbye. Another quick silent prayer was offered up for this most fortuitous blessing. The elite of San Angelo would be eating brisket after all.

23

I shifted my attention to the beans as I noted that the party was to commence in about a half-hour.

The phone in the lodge hangs on the wall just behind the kitchen. For the second time that morning, it rang. Once again, it was Toad. I was on pins and needles.

Bad news, Toad said. The barbecue place where I had sent him had no briskets. None whatsoever. They were completely sold out of everything.

Thinking quickly now, I told Toad to hurry to the Pack Saddle Bar-B-Que place out by the lake. Since it was Saturday, that joint was sure to have plenty of briskets. Ever ready to be helpful in this terrible crisis, once again Toad assured me he was "on it." One more prayer. Mercy. I was making a pest of myself with all these prayers.

Now I could see even more traffic passing by the lodge on the road to the river park. The party was only minutes away. I had the beans and the one, lone brisket ready to transport to the scene. All I lacked was the additional briskets Toad was to bring. I could slice them once we were at the river. Where the hell was Toad? All I could see in my mind's eye were the faces of San Angelo's most distinguished citizens awaiting me and those briskets down there at the river. I was a basket case.

Once again, the infamous phone rang. By now, that thing was as loud as a fire alarm. It was Toad.

Bad, bad, bad news. Toad, as instructed, had rushed to the Pack Saddle Bar-B-Que place out by the lake. His report hit me like a ton of bricks. They had no briskets. They had neither ribs nor sausage. The report could not have been grimmer. Or is it 'more grim'? Who cares? I was in one hell of a shape.

No runs. No hits. No errors. I was out of airspeed, altitude and ideas.

As I was talking on that lodge phone, looking through the kitchen out the front door of the lodge, I was trying to remember some barbecue place out on the north side of town. What are some of those names out that way? Any exploratory trip to the north side of town would take lots of time. My mind was blank. I couldn't think. Toad was pressing me for directives. I was helpless. Toad said he had tried every place I had suggested, all to no avail. The tool party was going to be a disaster without that brisket lunch. Most likely, every guest would keep his gift as a protest for the lunch fiasco and Devin would be tool-less. The groom would hold me responsible for the disaster. Toad was pressing for instructions on what to do next. Forever more, I would be an outcast in San Angelo remembered only as "No-Brisket Duncan."

And then it happened.

As I was on the phone to Toad and was looking helplessly out the front door of the lodge, I could see Toad, himself, pull up in his truck. He was talking on his cell phone. Yes, yes. He was talking to me on the lodge phone while he was right there in front of my eyes in his vehicle.

That scoundrel Toad has succeeded in buying the needed briskets at the first place I had sent him. From then on, he would call every ten minutes on his cell phone during his trip out to the ranch to report his next bulletin of misinformation. It had all been a giant trick he had played on me.

Toad had saved the day. But for pert-near an hour, I had thought that my life in San Angelo had come to an inglorious end. The party, thanks to Toad, was a success. Males, after all, can indeed contribute effectively to a wedding production. The guests had gifted Devin with lots of neat tools. I should have borrowed a big hammer to hit Toad over the head. But I needed to hug him first. Then I had to pay him for those briskets.

Oh, yeah. One other thing. Why were five of those original briskets not fit to eat? As I came to learn, it was – as usual – entirely my fault. Putting cooked meat while it is still warm into a freezer will ruin the meat. Being warm, meat will freeze improperly and leave an unpleasant taste. Yes, absolutely – it surely will. Damned unpleasant. I can testify to that piece of news. Live and learn.

The Perfect Whiskey

Toad and Sid Tucker were once members of a group of a dozen or so other couples who hosted a big annual party. There was plenty of food and drink, and the affair was topped off with a dandy outdoor dance which lasted until midnight.

A required admission fee to the shindig was a fifth of alcohol. This bounty was served to the guests. So obviously, the party was well supplied with many brands of spirits. There had to be, I supposed, plenty of bottles of booze left over after the last drink of the night had been poured.

Almost all the attendees would dutifully bring a decent bottle, but a few cheap scalawags would enter with the cheapest rot gut they could find. After the party was over, the hosts would divvy up the left-over supply. I always guessed that the bourbon drinkers in the group would swap and trade with the Scotch drinkers and so on. But I also imagined that each host would wind up with a proportionate share of the cut-rate stuff.

As we were preparing to go on a fishing trip one time, Toad took me to the building where he stored his bass boat. Once inside the unit, I took note of the boxes and boxes of fishing lures he had accumulated during his career as a bass fisherman. Stacked alongside were more boxes and boxes of alcohol which just had to be Toad's accumulated share of several years of hosting that party. Toad wasn't a big drinker, but he had a supply of alcohol of whatever he might choose to drink that would last several lifetimes.

One of those years along about then, Toad showed up out at my ranch right before Christmas. He proclaimed big news: He had a Christmas present for me. The two of us didn't normally exchange gifts for that holiday. I did, however, have a splendid deal worked out with Max Sanders, another of my good buddies. For Christmas, Max would buy me a case of my brand of beer, and I would reciprocate by purchasing a case of his favorite brew. What could beat a deal like that? But I had no such arrangement with Toad. What's up?

Now Toad was gifting me with a bottle of whiskey. He had it stashed away under the seat of his truck. I had done Toad no special favors lately, and I was struck by his gesture. As he handed it to me, I didn't recognize the brand. It was of an unknown origin. I'm not a particular connoisseur of whiskey, but I am familiar with the more recognizable labels.

"Skipper," Toad said as the bottle passed from his hand to mine, "this is a perfect whiskey for you."

Now I was really impressed. I imagined Toad had been shopping for something exotic, since he did, with his years of experience in hosting parties at cattlemen's conventions, probably know a lot more about whiskey than I did. Maybe it was some top-shelf brand found only on Wall Street or the U.S. Senate? In any case, that label did have the appearance of something expensive and rare, to my untrained eye anyway. What a magnanimous gesture on his part.

"Wow. Thanks, Toad," I replied. "But gosh, how do you know what would be a perfect whiskey for me?" I was still amazed by his insight.

"Here's the deal, Skipper, and why it's perfect for you," Toad admitted truthfully. "If it were any better whiskey,

I wouldn't be giving it to you. And if it was any worse, you couldn't drink it."

All of a sudden, the vision of all those piles of boxes of whiskey in Toad's boat storage barn flashed before my eyes. Rare indeed. Once again, I had been tricked by Toad. He could give me a bottle of liquor for Christmas for the rest of my life and never run out.

Let's all drink to Toad Tucker. And I just happen to have the perfect whiskey to pour the first toast.

Stories Collected from Rodeo Friends

Trappers

Conventional wisdom has it that the proliferation of varmints on West Texas ranches has exploded over the past couple of decades because so few people practice the skill of trapping anymore.

Oh, sure. A few craftsmen still play the game, but if you can believe what you hear, they are a rare breed these days. Years ago, it is said, when fair numbers of people lived and worked in the country, ranch hands would supplement their meager wages by trapping during the winter months. Back then, you could also find young outdoorsmen from town who would invest capital in traps hoping to increase their net worth. Almost all ranchers welcomed anyone who wanted to run a trap line.

The pelt of a raccoon or a ringtail promised ready cash, usually in short supply for almost all country folk. Fox hides (both red and grey) were even more of an incentive. Bobcats were, and continue to be, the ultimate prize. Come wintertime, there was great interest in the going price for the various hides. Just like any other commodity, the market fluctuated widely. The prime topic of conversation among those who dreamed of wealth from the fur business seemed to be "which buyer was paying what."

As a matter of interest, back in the days before the steep decline in sheep numbers, the vigorous trapping done by everyone kept the coyote population at almost zero in the heart of sheep country around San Angelo. Nowadays bounties are paid by various "trapping clubs" on these predators, but it is never enough to elicit widespread participation. If coyotes would fetch $1,000 each, they might wind up on the endangered species list.

At some point during the final decade of the last century, fur prices declined to the point that few trappers went to the trouble. It was Economics 101. When furs, for whatever reason, fell out of fashion, pelt prices tumbled. As it became impossible to cover expenses, traps were left in boxes in the barn. Varmint numbers seemed to increase exponentially.

During those days of low prices, and finding evidence of mischievous raccoons around the skinning shed at my hunting lodge, I placed a live trap to see if I could reduce coon numbers a bit. I caught over 30 of them in that many days. The little bandits can't resist Meow Mix. I finally quit because I grew weary of trans-locating the prisoners away from the temptations of the hunting headquarters.

But in days gone by when fur prices were quite lucrative, one of my old roping buddies, Bud Upton, even got himself in the game.

Bud and I had roped calves together, practicing either at his ranch or mine, on a more-or-less regular basis for a while. But Bud had more interest in steer roping and finally began to focus on that one event. For a variety of reasons, I never even considered roping steers, preferring instead to work on my calf roping skills. So it came to pass that Bud and I began to see less and less of each other as our respective paths led us apart. There is nothing unusual or threatening when old friends develop dissimilar hobbies. You just move on separately as you follow your new interests.

BUD UPTON

Bud succeeded in making a pretty darn good steer roper out of himself. He competed and won at some of the nation's most prestigious events. Bud was also the chairman of our local Fall Roping Fiesta and invited me to serve on that committee.

It was late winter in the early 1980s, and I had not seen Bud since the fall roping event back in early November. I ran into him one day, parked at the curb in front of a downtown store. His pickup did not look like it belonged to a rodeo hand or a rancher either – it was filled with buckets of traps and paraphernalia for mysterious uses. Dried blood and goo smeared the inside of the tailgate. I have recently come to learn that trappers haul more equipment than bow hunters or turkey hunters combined. Bud was living proof of that. You could hardly cram one more tool into the bed of his long wheelbase truck.

"Good grief, Bud," I implored. "What in the world is all this stuff?" I was more used to seeing saddles, feed sacks, bridles and ropes. Other than the multitude of steel traps, I hardly recognized anything. "What in the hell have you been doing?" It was obvious what he had been doing, but I wanted details.

"Trapping varmints." Intuitively, he knew his questioner was a rank amateur in need of basic instruction. Thankfully, Bud was a patient professor.

"My, my, my," was all I could say as I marveled at the vast array of gidgets and gadgets. "Trapping, eh? I've heard that fur prices are mighty high this year, so I guess it is a good time to get into the trade." I didn't even pause as I continued to voice my thoughts out loud. "I didn't know you were this much of a trapper. I'll bet there is a lot to learn. Have you caught very many critters? Are you harvesting enough pelts to make it worth your while? It must take a lot of time to get into the deal in a big way."

And then I hit him with the really big question that was on my mind. "Wow, Bud. Are you any good at trapping?"

"Well, Skipper," Bud began earnestly, "let me tell you a story, and then you tell me if I'm any good at trapping." And with this bulletin as a headline, he began his tale - - -

"The other day, I was driving around on my ranch – on a road I have traveled thousands of times with ranching on my mind – when all of a sudden, now thinking mostly about trapping, I spotted a game trail coming down a fence by a field. There was another trail coming from the other direction and both intersected right in front of a big bush which had a perfect hidey-hole right next to the junction of the trails. I had never seen a better place to put a trap.

"Right away, I stopped my truck and reached into the back for just the size trap I wanted. I also grabbed up my 5 gallon bucket which contained all my trapping gear. Stuffed in this container were the cotton gloves I always wear when setting a trap. You know, of course, that cotton gloves don't leave any telltale scent to warn off a varmint. (No, I didn't know this fact.)

"Also in the bucket was a length of canvas which I unrolled to work off of as I dug the hole for the trap. Once again, the canvas helps conceal my scent from any passing varmint.

"So just at the entrance to that cave in the thorn bush, I dug a small hole with my gloved hands. I set the trap, taking care not to get caught in the thing myself, and placed it carefully into the depression. I then used a sifter I made to sprinkle the loose dirt in and around the trap. When I got that done, you couldn't tell a trap was even there. It lay perfectly buried below that loose soil and was totally invisible. The trap had a length of chain which I similarly buried and secured to the nearby bush. Any varmint would find it impossible to run away with my trap."

Bud continued with his tale as I hung on every word.

"Finally, but most importantly, I found my bottle of special scent. Trappers use genuine varmint urine because it is a powerful attractant. I'm a huge believer in the stuff. Using the enclosed eye dropper, I put just three drops of that distinct odoriferous elixir about 8 inches behind that hidden trap. Any passing varmint couldn't help but stop to "read the newspaper" with his nose. He would simply, positively, have to check out this new odor in his domain. To do so, he'd surely step right into my trap. So there I had, to my mind anyway, a perfect set. I looked it all over one last time just be sure I got it all right. I backed off my canvas cloth and rolled it up, removed my cotton gloves, put everything back into the bucket, loaded it in my truck and headed on down the road. No doubt, I would harvest a valuable pelt from this effort."

I was all ears, listening to Bud's account of his adventure to this point. Much of what he'd talked about was brand new to me, and I was already learning a lot I didn't know about trapping. After a respectable pause to catch his breath and to collect his thoughts, Bud went on with his tale.

"As it so happened," Bud continued, "there is a guy working on the ranch who is driving a bulldozer pushing brush for us. Just like me, this cat skinner (as bulldozer drivers are affectionately called) has an interest in trapping and is pretty good at it. He catches plenty of critters."

I stood there, mute, waiting for the story to continue.

"A couple of days later," Bud went on, "this guy was headed to the bulldozer in his truck traveling that same ranch road I had been on. All of a sudden, he saw something of great interest, especially to a trapper. He spotted a game trail coming down a fence by a field. There was another trail coming from the other direction. Both intersected right in front of a big bush which had a perfect hidey-hole right next to the junction of the trails. He had never seen a better place to place a trap. He even saw some fox scat right there in the road. He quickly concluded that I would surely have a trap somewhere in that promising area.

"Wouldn't it be something," he mused, "if I caught a varmint right in old Bud's honey hole?" The dream consumed his thoughts.

"So immediately, he stopped his truck, which, like mine, is cluttered with all kinds of trapping gear. He began to consider what kind of trap might be the perfect size for a set of this kind. He, too, uses a 5-gallon bucket to hold all his gear. Getting everything together, he spotted a perfect location for his trap, right next to that thorn bush with the cavernous hole. In the bottom of his bucket, he found his cotton gloves and put them on both hands before he touched anything, especially the trap. With this closer look, he was convinced he had found an ideal location. He carefully unrolled his canvas so he would leave no scent while he worked. He kneeled on the cloth and studied the ground closely."

Bud paused for effect to allow my slow mind to catch up to the events in the saga.

"Now it was time to dig the hole with his hand. It appeared the dirt where he wanted his trap was already pretty soft and the digging would be easy."

At this point, I could envision the climax of Bud's story. It wasn't going to be pretty. Or painless, either.

The next day, Bud ran his trap line and when he arrived at his new set, he quickly noted that things were amiss. The ground appeared mightily disturbed as if a varmint might have pulled out of the trap. But wonder of wonders – the trap was still set, although it was covered poorly. What in the world?

In making his rounds, Bud happened to check on the bulldozer project. The driver seemed ill at ease and could hardly look Bud in the eye. To clear his conscience, he finally made a full confession. His attempted prank backfired on him in a disastrous way. He bared his soul and revealed the horrid details of that trick gone bad.

Bud concluded his tale thusly: "My trap got him just about where his fingers tie onto his hand. Thank goodness he was wearing those gloves. He didn't get hurt all that bad." I winced at the thought of a steel trap slamming shut across my hand, cotton glove or no glove.

Bud did get in a good jibe at the now-shamed trickster. He politely asked the sheepish villain if he got hurt when he hit the end of that chain.

Bud assured me that the victim finally made a full recovery.

"So," Bud concluded his tale in a most memorable manner. "You ask if I'm doing any good with my trapping, here's what I say:

"You can call yourself a trapper when you've trapped another trapper."

That kind of proof ought to stand up in any court.

Bear Attack

Back in the 1950s, Texas and Oklahoma calf ropers would head north to the easy pickings at rodeos held during the summer months in the Rocky Mountains. Why were events for calf ropers easy to win? It was said that the northern cowboys dominated the bronc-riding events, but few of them could rope as good as the Southwesterners. And why was this supposed to be a fact? The inclement weather of the northern states kept those far-north ropers from the year-round practice needed to hone their skills.

On the other hand, rough-stock riders dominated the horse-pitching events because of the proliferation of draft horses needed for the vast haying operations demanded by northern cattle operations. Moreover, the northern ranges held respectable numbers of wild mustangs. Cowboys in those parts were forever catching and breaking feral horses to supplement their income.

So Texans and Okies won the calf ropings and the Northern boys won the bareback and saddle bronc events. Bronc riding was a tradition up north. Roping calves was the ritual in the Southwest. Nowadays, of course, champion ropers or riders are liable to come from any corner of the nation. No doubt, modern indoor arenas which aid year-round practice have contributed to this fact.

In the mid-1960s when I had returned home from college to live and work on our family ranch, my hobby and passion was calf roping. Almost every weekend, a jackpot roping would be held within easy driving distance. If all possible, I would show up for the contest. The entry fees were affordable and competing against other ropers under pressure when timed with a stopwatch was more beneficial than simply practicing my skills at home.

The jackpot ropings (no money was added to the purse; only the participants' entry fees were at stake) attracted not only us rank amateurs, but we had to compete against wily veterans who had years of experience at the sport. It was a fruitful learning environment. Some of these "old-timers" were 10-20 years older and had competed at many rodeos over the years. They were the professors; I was the eager student.

One of the most memorable of these guys was Bill Jones. Standing about 6 feet tall, but lean and wiry, he was a cowboy athlete for sure. Moreover, he was a superb horse trainer and generous with tips about keeping the performance of a roping horse sharp. Bill had actually "rodeoed up north" for years and was a wealth of information on the entire sport. He had done it all, and I always enjoyed the tales of his experiences on the rodeo trail. The best story he told was this one:

Sometime back in the 1950s, Bill and his traveling companion, Jiggs Burk, spent the summer entering calf-roping events in the northern mountain states. Jiggs was a member of the famous Burk family from Oklahoma which has produced a number of great calf ropers over the decades.

BILL JONES

Yes, they went north for the prize money but in order to return home with sufficient capital to carry them through the winter, they traveled and lived very frugally. The two calf ropers camped out every night, sleeping on cots and cooking most of their own meals. Their mode of transportation was far simpler than what is in use by today's rodeo crowd. They had only a basic pickup and a side-by-side two-horse trailer.

In their wildest dreams, they could never have imagined today's giant trucks and four-horse trailers equipped with fancy, air-conditioned living quarters. The huge rigs you see now were unheard of back then. Nope, these mid-century calf ropers were living much like their forefathers of the century before who traversed the west in ox-drawn wagons. To be sure, the two "modern" cowboys covered many more miles per day with that 1950s model truck.

Their side-by-side horse trailer had a compartment for saddles and gear under the front of the trailer. It was situated just under the feed bin where the horses could nibble at their grain as they made their long journeys between the far-flung rodeos. The two cowboys would scrutinize the latest issue of "Rodeo Sports News" to set their agenda of travel. The challenge was to get to as many rodeos as possible with logistics, distance and time always a factor in their decisions.

All-night drives were common and, of course, they needed to find a phone somewhere to get entered at the chosen contests. Just getting an open line to a rodeo secretary might take hours hanging around a pay phone somewhere. Their focus was on the smaller events where the competition was easier. They mostly stayed away from the larger, more well-known rodeos such as Cheyenne.

So there they were, Bill and Jiggs, somewhere in southwestern Montana. Thankfully, at the moment they had plenty of time to get to the next rodeo on their agenda and both looked forward to a decent night's sleep there at their trailer. Campgrounds in the forest were not hard to find, and they couldn't imagine a more beautiful place to spend the night. But when they sought directions to a likely place from a forest ranger, he cautioned them about bears. Yep, he said, bears were abundant in the area, and they need to be aware of that fact. Good grief. Neither the Okie nor the Texan had any experience with bears. It was a brand new threat. They listened closely to the admonitions of the ranger and made plenty of mental notes. Upon their departure from that particular advisor, and as they followed his directions to a likely camping spot, they discussed possible defensive measures to deal with this new challenge. Mercy. Bears. Nothing came close to that back home.

Instead of sleeping on their old army cots under the starlit sky as usual, their plan was to lay out their bedrolls on the floor of that side-by-side horse trailer. Using pine limbs as brooms, they succeeded in sweeping out most of the horse manure. They tied each roping horse to opposite sides of the trailer and took care to hang a feed bucket nearby. They had watered the ponies at a clear mountain stream just before dark.

As they rolled out their canvas bedrolls on the floor of the trailer, conversation between the two dealt mainly with bears. Neither had ever even seen one. What are their habits? Are they aggressive? Do they attack humans without provocation? They had many more questions than answers.

With neither pistol nor rifle in their gear, having some kind of protection against a bear attack seemed to be a good idea. In considering several choices, Bill found an effective weapon. He armed himself with a cot stay. With both ropers sleeping inside the horse trailer, there was insufficient room to set up their cots. So the strong wooden rod used to hold apart the sides of the old army cots would not be used. The cot stay was a logical choice. Bill lost no time in extracting the new weapon from one of their idle cots.

Practice-swinging the thing around like a baseball bat, Bill judged it would give him a decent chance if a bear attack did, indeed, come during the night. Those cot sticks, made of oak, are plenty strong and surely wouldn't break, even with the most violent swing. Yep, he was safe and secure with that cot stay.

Finally, after their supper around a small campfire, the two ropers took to their beds laid out there on the floor of the trailer, still talking mostly about bears. It had been a busy day. Both were plenty worn out from their countless miles of travel, and blessed sleep came upon the pair fairly quickly.

Now, it was way into the night. Easy snoring had provided most of the night sounds around the trailer. But things were about to change, big time.

From a deep sleep, Jiggs was suddenly, instantly awake. Quickly aware of his new surroundings, he knew intuitively that something wasn't right. He sensed danger. Slowly, in the dim moonlight, his eyes adjusted to the dark conditions. Looking up from the floor toward the rear of the horse trailer silhouetted against the night sky, he was alarmed to see the outline of a bear, peering over the rear door into their bedroom. His heart immediately jumped right into his throat. His pulse quickened. By now he was as wide awake as a tree full of owls.

Having made no preparations with a weapon of any kind, Jiggs poked the still-sleeping Bill and stage-whispered "BEAR." In his confusion, no other plan seemed to make sense.

Was it the poke, or the word "bear?" No matter. In either case, Bill came quickly to his senses, thankful that he had taken the precaution of arming himself with that cot stick. As a man of action, he knew exactly what he was going to do. Before falling asleep, he had rehearsed the plan. Grabbing his weapon in both hands, and slowly, slowly raising himself to a kneeling position to face the rear of the trailer and this alarming threat, Bill drew a bead on his target. He hammered down as hard as he possibly could, right smack across the head of that bear. That would do it for sure. They would be saved.

But it wasn't a bear. It was Bill's roping horse who had dozed off as he stood there, resting his head on the gate of the trailer.

There was only one predictable outcome. The poor, startled horse set back so violently that he broke his halter to smithereens. Away he ran, loose in that vast forest in the middle of the night.

Instantly remorseful, Bill was aghast at what he'd done. His faithful horse had been pounded over the head for no reason. As he heard the fleeting hoof beats growing dimmer and dimmer with the horse running flat-out down the slope of the road into oblivion, Bill was sick to his stomach. His horse was sometimes difficult to bridle in a corral. How would he ever succeed in catching him in this endless forest? Especially now that his old pal would be extra-leery of Bill and a possible warp over the head with a cot stay?

Jiggs was busy calming his own horse which, naturally, was plenty upset himself about this turn of events. A tethered horse is always distressed when his pal is running wild and free. Bill continued to berate himself over his senseless act. He'd never win another dime up north, and he wished he was back home.

But the story has a happy ending. As it turned out, there were, indeed, bears in that forest, just as the ranger had said. Bill's horse ran and ran until, finally exhausted, he stopped long enough to catch his breath. Which caused him to smell bears.

Horses, it is said, are instinctively and deathly afraid of bears. As luck would have it, Bill's frightened horse immediately returned to the only place where he really felt at home – next to that trailer that had been his sanctuary for the past several weeks. After the unbearably long wait and berating himself the entire time, Bill couldn't believe his ears. There was no mistake. Approaching hoof sounds. When Bill saw his horse coming, his joy knew no bounds. His old partner came up to him in a spirit of forgiveness and eagerly put his head right into the awaiting and now repaired halter. The horse was safe from bears. Bill had his old buddy back. Life is good. Just wait till the next rodeo. We'll show 'em. Probably win the whole shindig, too.

It is said that all's well that ends well. The two ropers finally returned home late that summer, their jeans jingling with cash and ready to sleep in a real bed for a change. There is no doubt about it. Both were thankful there are no bears in Texas or Oklahoma.

Everything Just Went Blank

One of my favored spots for roping contests was Mason, Texas. About once a month, they would host a calf roping and team roping on a Sunday afternoon. It wasn't a complicated affair – you would simply enter when you got there. When the beleaguered secretaries finally got everyone tabulated, roping activities would get under way. Almost always, calf ropers would go first. And again, the organizers usually scheduled two go-rounds for both events. So the format would be the first round of calf roping followed by the first round of team roping. When that concluded, the calf contestants would rope, or try to rope, their second calf of the day. The last round of the team roping would conclude the day. The jackpot money would be divvied up three ways with an equal amount in each of the two go-rounds and the "average," a misnomer for the total time on two head.

If time allowed, and usually it did, a quick one go-round contest would conclude the day's activities.

One memorable Sunday, the first round of the calf roping had concluded. We calf ropers were watching the first round of the team roping. Of course, several cowboys would enter both events.

For quite some time, I had been squatting like a baseball catcher (back in the days when I could do such) there by the bucking chutes, that being the best vantage point to (a) watch the team roping and (b) stay the hell out of the way and not get run over. Yes, yes, we spectators should have seated ourselves in the grandstands, but they were on the far side of the arena and who wants to walk that far just to watch a roping?

So there I squatted. Finally, the announcer noted that only three teams remained in the go-round. He instructed the calf ropers to be ready for their second round. I remembered that I was to rope early, so I needed to get busy. I quickly stood up to go retrieve my horse tied somewhere outside the arena.

Suddenly, as I gained my full height, everything went black. Although it was a sunny, bright day, it seemed as if the lights had gone totally out during the night. With both eyes wide open, I could see nothing. I later learned that when you've been in a squatting position for a length of time, and when you suddenly stand up, all your blood runs to both legs, depriving your eyes of the fluid which makes vision possible.

Completely blinded now, and all of a sudden losing my balance, I remembered seeing another roper nearby. I stumbled for a couple of steps in his direction with both my arms out to try to catch on to any support I could find to keep from falling. I succeeded in grabbing hold of the roper, my arms encircling his shoulders.

Just then, my vision slowly returned and things began to come in to focus. I was horrified to see that I was holding on to one of the most gruff, inhospitable, cranky contestants in the entire park. His name shall remain anonymous because he still lives and would kill me if he found his name in this book.

"What the hell are you doing? Turn me loose," he ordered. "Right now."

I began an effusive apology. "Gosh," I confessed, "I just stood up there too quickly, and everything went dark. I couldn't see anything. I was afraid I'd fall."

Just then, an inspiration came to me. I endeavored to seek his sympathy by asking, "Did anything like that ever happen to you?"

Only mildly amused now by my misfortune, he came back with a ready answer to my query.

"Heck yes," he remembered. "I've had that happen plenty of times out there at the Boots and Saddles Club in San Angelo."

In those days, that dance hall and beer joint drew the largest crowds in West Texas.

Billy Hogan

I first got to know Billy Hogan at the monthly jackpot ropings at Mason, Texas. He was a team roper. I rarely entered that event, preferring instead to focus on calf roping. Once I got to know him, I always looked forward to seeing Billy anywhere on the rodeo trail.

With his unhurried manner of speaking and his easy-going ways, it was incongruous that such a slow-mover as Billy Hogan would willingly participate in a contest where the winner is determined by a stop watch. Billy's non-roping friends could never imagine him hurrying at anything. But he loved team roping and was pretty darn good at it, despite his lack of haste in anything else.

Truly, there never was a prettier spot as Mason for a roping arena. Huge trees with plenty of shade made it easy to find a place to park your rig. And the dirt in that pen, while not quite sandy, was a mellow, loamy soil that was perfect for our cowboy purposes.

What made Mason special, however, was Billy Hogan. Before the day's competition would get under way, Billy would treat any interested music lover to a concert with his fiddle. As the ropers were saddling horses and arranging their gear, Billy would find a shady spot to play his music. With a guitar player such as John Burrus from Indian Gap as his only accompaniment, he would rip off an impressive array of tunes. Not only could he bring a tear to your eye with any of the old Texas dance hall favorites such as "Faded Love" or "Maiden's Prayer", he would also throw in one of those complicated melodies favored by participants in fiddle contests where you'd hear an array of intricate chord changes.

It was inconceivable to me that a fiddle player such as Billy would even consider taking up team roping. When team ropers catch either the horns or the heels of a steer, their dallies of the rope around the saddle horn (always wrapped with rubber to increase friction) to turn or stop a steer are fraught with hazards for the ropers' fingers. No doubt, when you find yourself in a collection of team ropers, there will be a few in the group who can't produce 10 digits. Billy paid no attention to these inherent dangers. He loved to rope steers, and he loved to play his fiddle. And that was that.

My first and most cherished love was bluegrass music played by such artists as Flatt and Scruggs or the Stanley Brothers. It was rare to hear any bluegrass in Texas in those days. In 1969, Joe Henderson, another devotee of that style of mountain music, and I attended the first-ever bluegrass music festival held west of the Mississippi in Hugo, Oklahoma. To say we were smitten would hardly describe our elation. So I began touting that event at every opportunity to anyone who might be interested. I must have done a pretty good sales job because the next year, Billy Hogan, Wade Choate and Terry Sinclair went along as I returned to the event in Hugo. Like Joe and me the year before, all the West Texans were mesmerized by the scores of jam sessions to be found in the camping area at Hugo.

Up until that event, Billy had never been exposed to much bluegrass music, and that style of fiddling was not yet in his repertoire. But when Billy heard those bluegrass fiddle players just that one time, it wasn't long until he had added plenty of bluegrass tunes to his playlist. He was a natural at any kind of fiddle playing, take your pick. After some period of time, Billy joined some other talented pickers from the Hill Country to form the "Poverty Playboys." With bib overalls as their stage dress, they were a hit at every appearance they made. The group even received a standing ovation at a Berea, Kentucky festival when their band followed the legendary Bill Monroe who had received only polite applause. No doubt about it – Billy Hogan was one talented fiddle player.

As I got ever more into the music scene, I began to host pickings at the river park on my ranch attended by West Texas devotees of bluegrass. Billy would come often, and he could hold his own with anyone. He was a master at those super-fast instrumental breakdowns in the jam sessions. The different styles of fiddle music are unappreciated by many music lovers. Just because a fiddler can play dance hall music doesn't necessarily mean he can play bluegrass. Or vice-versa. Contest fiddle tunes are an entirely different specialty. Billy Hogan was dad-gummed good at all of them. Thankfully, to my tastes anyway, I never heard him attempt any violin concertos.

As time went on, I had virtually quit roping and saw less and less of Billy at Mason and other roping venues. My hobby of roping had waned. My new hobby was trying to learn to play the banjo.

So, a period of time had passed – a year or two maybe, or was it longer? Anyway, I had planned another gathering of musicians for a shindig down on the river and I called Billy to alert him about the pending event. In fact, his name was at the top of my list of invitees. When I finally tracked him down, he had big news. I couldn't believe my ears. Billy had recently undergone a heart transplant.

All this happened back in the days before that particular operation became semi-commonplace. Indeed, to that time, there had been few of the procedures done anywhere. Billy revealed that he received his new heart in a hospital in San Antonio, not all that far from his home in Harper, Texas. He assured me that he was now recovered sufficiently to be able to attend the picking. He would fill me in on the details of his surgery when he arrived.

I could hardly wait to hear his story, even though I knew it would take him as long to tell it as it took to happen. Being brief was not one of Billy's traits. Each sentence out of his mouth was repeated as an instant replay. Two sentences for the price of one, just to be sure you got the message. And his super-slow manner of speech only exacerbated the deal. You didn't want to start a conversation with Billy if you sensed an impending trip to the bathroom.

Come to find out, when he showed up for the music event, not only did he have a new heart, he also had now taken a wife. He and Gail, another Hill Country girl and the sister of one of his team roping partners, had married just before his surgery. Up to this time anyway, what with his roping and his music, he had never had time to find a mate.

In addition to his roping skills and his fiddle-playing talents, Billy had an ornery streak. For example, he and his bride, Gail, had moved her waterbed into their home. Billy, to be properly prepared for the night, showed up at bedtime wearing goggles and flippers.

GAIL AND BILLY HOGAN

Before the hardcore music finally commenced later on that afternoon there by the river, Billy gave me the full history of his heart surgery. It was a fascinating tale.

Unbeknownst to me, Billy had suffered from a congenital heart situation for years. He was a perfect candidate for a transplant. The pioneers in heart-transplant surgery had found Billy – or maybe it was the other way around. The details are not important to the story. Somehow, Billy was the beneficiary of the new science. All the preliminary work had been done, a date for the procedure was set, and Billy wound up with a brand new heart. He said his hospital stay, in those days when the tissue-rejection issues were at the top of the patient's list of problems, ran to several weeks. After the surgery, the doctors visited Billy almost every day to check on his progress.

Remember, I said that Billy had a penchant for mischief. While in the hospital, he was a model patient, to be sure, but he couldn't help himself. In his crowd, pranks were the name of the game. Cowboys, especially, are among the worst practitioners of shenanigans.

Several days post-surgery during his doctor's visit, Billy assumed a very serious demeanor. He pressed his doctor for exact details on his recent procedure.

"Doc," asked Billy in a very solemn manner, "as I understand it, you took my own heart completely out of my chest. With that thing now out of the way, you then placed another heart in its place. Is that correct?"

Unsure of just where this line of questioning might be headed, the doctor replied, "Why, yes, Billy. That is exactly what we did."

Now that the doctor had nibbled at his bait, Billy went on with his query. Not having anything else to do with his time, he was enjoying stringing the poor physician along.

"So you removed my entire heart out of my chest. It's gone. It's out of there." The doctor kept nodding affirmatively as Billy detailed all the recent history. Finally, Billy got to the point he had been working up to all along.

"I'm wondering, Doc. What happened to my old heart? What did you guys do with it?"

The poor doctor's alarm bells were now ringing. He was trapped in a line of questioning he did not want to follow. To be sure, he knew the answer to that question, but frankly it was none of anyone's business what had happened to that old heart.

As everyone knows, the best answer to an unwanted question is to ask a question in reply. So the doctor, cautious as could be, replied warily: "Now Billy, why do you need to know that?"

With a twinkle in his eye, Billy sprang his trap on the doctor. "Well, Doc, if you still have my old heart stored away somewhere, when I finally get out of the hospital, I thought that thing might be good bait to put on a trot line."

In those early transplant days, heart patients stayed near the hospital for weeks as their condition and rejection situations were closely monitored. Billy enjoyed decent progress and it wasn't long until he was allowed more and more freedom.

Billy's heart surgeon, Dr. Charles Moore, owned some park-like property close to the hospital. One nice spring day, Dr. Moore hosted a gala event at the venue for his transplant recipients and their families. In addition to the huge picnic, a country band had been hired. Billy instructed Gail to bring his fiddle to the event, just in case. Sure enough, after the band had played a few tunes, Billy asked to sit in with the group. With Billy's prowess with that fiddle, he quickly stole the show.

His signature song was "Pop Goes the Weasel", and Billy could play that tune on his fiddle behind his back, upside down, holding the bow between his knees, and several other ways that are impossible to describe. Children, especially, loved to watch Billy's antics with his instrument.

Dr. Moore, upon hearing Billy's incredible music, had no idea his patient was blessed with this kind of talent. Together with all the rest of those in attendance at the event, the surgeon stood there in awe as he watched the performance. Despite his easygoing demeanor, Billy morphed into a real showman when he played his fiddle. Beyond just his technical musical skills, Billy was an entertainer at heart. He couldn't help himself – he would dance a jig there on stage while making his music.

But now having been exposed for many weeks to Billy and his jolly-good jokes, the devious heart transplant surgeon lost no time in taking advantage of what he had just seen unfold there on the stage.

As the event came to an end, Dr. Moore took the microphone and announced to the audience some startling news.

He grew very serious as he told the assembled crowd that prior to Billy's heart transplant, Billy had never even tried to play a fiddle.

Billy loved it. And he appropriated that classic line every chance he got.

Tragically, Billy lived only a couple of years after his surgery. During all the procedures, he had unfortunately received a transfusion of blood tainted with Hepatitis C which prevented the use of most effective anti-rejections drugs. What a heartbreak.

Few people who ever knew Billy ever forgot him. Including me.

Fist Fights

To hear my dad tell it, finding a nice fist fight was the only reason he and his friends ever attended a dance or a party back in the 1920s and '30s. Indeed, many of Dad's pals from that era assured me that my father was quite a scrapper. I never saw this side of him. He exhibited no violence in my presence, and I could only marvel at the tales told of his pugilistic experiences.

History books suggest that fistfights were very, very common back during the frontier days in West Texas. But gun battles made all the news. Many such firefights became legendary. Almost anybody can name several of them. But apparently back then, fistfights were as common as house flies – hardly worth a mention in the news of the day.

As I seem to understand things, fist fighting continued to be practiced over the next few decades. In my youth, I never experienced a serious fight, but there were rumors of plenty of them among the "older" crowd – those boys who were six to eight years my senior. As sixth graders, we had all heard of several high school toughs in town. Their names were as well-known in our circles as famous baseball players in the major leagues. Reputedly, any of these guys could whip anyone they chose. And if they were unsuccessful in finding a victim somewhere, they would fight each other just for the practice. Yes, they would even fight among themselves for grins. Everyone in my crowd had heard of this remarkable trait, and no one questioned its legitimacy.

The rumor was, and all my amigos believed it without question, that if any one of us sixth graders happened to get caught by this high school crowd, they would take us out on the road to Arden west of town and make us take off our pants before releasing us to make our way home, embarrassed beyond belief. We all lived in dread of this calamity.

But despite the stories and rumors of frequent battles, I never personally saw a fight. I had heard of them among the high school crowd to be sure, and I had no doubt that such events occurred. But it was all hearsay. I could not truthfully testify as a witness if I might be called to the stand.

By the time I finally got to high school, fist fighting was on a steep decline. The ruffians of a few years ago were long gone. Their younger brothers, if they had them, were quite peaceful and docile. I always wondered why this was so. Did it have something to do with the fact that those older guys were born and reared in the heart of the Great Depression when both jobs and money were in short supply? My peers, born around the beginning of WW II, had life much easier as things began to boom in the war economy.

Those town brawlers with their violent tendencies all settled down (mostly) to become solid citizens. In later years, I came to know several of them. By then, they seemed to be quiet, gentle, kind men. Who would ever know? But while in their presence during the modern era, I could never quite forget their former, fearsome reputations.

Once I found myself in high school, a rumor of a big fight would be the topic on everyone's lips for a few days every now and then, but again, I was never a spectator at anything of the kind.

After college, and as I began to become infatuated with calf roping and rodeos, there was talk of fist fights among that crowd. Steer wrestlers, being the largest and brawniest of the cowboys, were supposed to be the worst for violence. I would hear of epic encounters and horrific fights occasionally, but of course, I never witnessed anything of the sort. Among my calf-roping companions, there were a few who were thought to be exceptionally ferocious, but when I was around them at the various roping contests and rodeos, I never saw anything to suggest latent streaks of violence. To a man, every one of them was pleasant to me. For which I was thankful.

So despite being well-situated over several years to witness a sho'nuff fistfight, I had never seen one. Not that I particularly wanted to, you understand, but when such stories arose among beer-drinking conversationalists around a campfire somewhere, I could only participate as a listener. Having never, ever seen a knock-down, drag-out battle, I had no eyewitness tale of my own to share.

And then I went to a rodeo at Post, Texas.

Post lies just under the Caprock, about 40 miles south of Lubbock. For miles and miles around that Texas Tech town, the land is as flat as a pool table. But the elevation change between Post and those plains is dramatic and sharp. The scenery is spectacular. Every summer, Post puts on one heck of an amateur rodeo. I even tied for first in the calf roping there one year with Jack Kirkpatrick, a former football star at Texas Tech. You are most likely to return to those contests where you might have won something in a prior year. So Post was a special favorite, and I always tried to enter if at all possible.

One year on my annual trek, as I pulled my rig into the contestant's parking area late that afternoon, I just happened to park alongside the truck and trailer owned by J.L. Sawyer from Garden City. He and his team roping partner had almost finished saddling their horses and would be headed toward the arena momentarily.

J.L. was a fearsome-looking guy. Being about 15 years older than me, he could have been an NFL lineman. Built square as a blockhouse, he would easily crush the life out of most anyone, I supposed. So naturally, I always took pains to be affable to him. I doubt he knew me from Adam, and I surely never wanted to incur his wrath. I was simply in awe of his fearsome looks and his tough reputation. And there I was parked right next to him at the Post rodeo.

I unloaded my horse and began to get my gear organized, taking care to stay the hell out of J.L.'s way. Had I known I would be next door to the ferocious-looking J.L. Sawyer when I pulled up to park, I would have selected a different spot. But it was too late for that move now, and I would just have to take special care in minding my own business.

By now, J.L. had mounted his horse and was headed to the arena, his nylon rope hanging from his saddle horn. We were both parked facing the driveway road which encircled the outside of the arena. Vehicles were coming and going, but being parked head-on to that road would be handy for a quick getaway once our contesting time was over. We wouldn't get penned in by the scattered parked vehicles and unable to leave when we wanted.

As I saddled my horse, J.L. rode across the road in a slow walk. He was headed to the arena to exercise and slow-lope his team-roping horse. Just as he was almost across that narrow road, an approaching car came near to hitting him, or rather, to colliding with his horse. The nimble animal quickly dodged out of the way and almost bolted out from under J.L. in the process. The car hadn't been moving particularly fast, but a near-collision was luckily avoided. Maybe the driver had been distracted by something.

Understandably angry at the carelessness of the driver, J.L. hollered over his shoulder:

"Watch where you're going, you blind S.O.B." Except he didn't use the initials. Every word was spoken in a loud, threatening voice.

According to the lessons given me by my father, and from my reading of history, charging someone with being the offspring of a female dog was always, positively guaranteed to start a fight. Right there in front of my eyes, the epithet had been used in a belligerent manner. Anyone nearby could have heard the words. I wasn't 10 yards from the scene of the crime, and the charge rang in my ears. Already, no doubt, J.L.'s blood pressure had exploded. Just that quick, he was mad as hell.

And then it happened. The car skidded to a stop in a cloud of dust. The door swung open and out stepped a man who was, trust me on this one, even bigger and meaner looking than J.L. Sawyer. Oh mercy, me oh my. An eruption was under way and I would be a witness to history.

Gaining his full height now, the driver of the car shouted at the man on the dun horse he had almost hit:

"What did you say to me?" His fists were already doubled. I couldn't believe my eyes. I had a front row seat for a heavyweight, world championship fight.

Wheeling his horse around now, and stepping off the pony with his back to the car driver, J.L. shouted over his shoulder:

"I said watch where you are going, you blind S.O.B." His voice was full of venom. Now that his feet were solidly on the ground, J.L. turned to face his opponent. The car driver was scampering to meet him somewhere in the middle of that road. They rushed together, face to face, at the back of that car and right in front of me. My horse and my saddle were forgotten. The unfolding scene was beyond belief.

J.L., now with his fists also doubled and ready to go, raised his head to face his opponent. He was astonished at what he saw. It took a moment or two for the realization to come, which seemed like an hour to me.

"Pete," he said merrily as he recognized a long-lost buddy.

"J.L.," crooned Pete. It was obvious that neither had seen the other in years.

They embraced each other and hugged with what could only be described as brotherly love. The value of my front-row, 50-yard line, ringside seat (I love mixed metaphors) at the spectacle of the century went suddenly to zero. Who wants to pay to see a cheerful reunion between two old farts?

The pair kept laughing about the near miss and blessing each other with sarcastic but fun-loving comments. Slapping each other on the back and hooting about the entire situation, their elation at finally finding each other knew no bounds. Both were as happy as a couple of puppies.

So that's as close as I've come to seeing a real fight. Being much older now and running with a peace-loving crowd, my chances of seeing a possible heavyweight battle are next to zip. But that's OK. And for sure, I don't want to be a participant myself.

WEST TEXAS LINGO

MAX TANKERSLEY

Just west of San Angelo and Tom Green County is Irion County. Pronounced "Erie-un," the area has produced an impressive array of characters. One of the most memorable was Max Tankersley.

Max was a rancher all his life, but back in the days when the sheep industry was dominant in West Texas, Max supplemented his ranching income with plenty of outside work, the most rigorous of which was drenching sheep for other livestock owners. You talk about hard work! Hardly any ranch chore comes close to that one.

Sheep, grazing as they do very close to the ground, are vulnerable to ingesting eggs of stomach worms. These pests cause weight loss, poor performance, and in extreme cases, even death. So sheep need to be drenched on a regular basis to keep their digestive systems free of stomach worms. Wet years demanded more trips through the drenching alley than did the dry times. Years ago, when Max first began his drenching career, the only effective "medicine" was phenothiazine. Having the consistency of a milk shake, the concoction was brutal not only to the worms and to the sheep themselves, but also to the drenching crew. The liquid gave off toxic fumes, so noxious that the fluid could only be contained and shipped in 1-gallon glass containers. The mixture was transferred to a small bucket for easy withdrawal by the tool used to drench the sheep.

A drenching crew was ideally composed of four men. The leader, Max, handled the giant stainless steel syringe with its 4-6-inch spout which was inserted into the mouth of each sheep to receive the dose well back and force swallowing. In a working alley full of sheep, two helpers would alternate in spinning the sheep around to face Max. As each animal was treated, it would run to the other end of the alley to join similarly treated mates. The third helper would be situated outside the alley holding the bucket of drench. Each dose had to be drawn up from the bucket for each sheep. The crew of three would switch places after every alley-full to give each other a break from catching and holding those heavy sheep. Being the bearer of the bucket, obviously, was the easiest chore. But poor Max got no break because his role was to drench every individual in the alley. When that particular batch was done, they would be released and the alley would be filled with new sheep. Hundreds of woolies could be drenched in one day. This brutal work would go on day after day during the season when stomach worms were prevalent.

MAX TANKERSLEY

What made phenothiazine so bad was the fumes it gave off. After even an hour or two of exposure to the liquid in that open bucket, your face would begin to blister as if you had incurred severe sunburn. A day or two later, your skin would actually peel off. Those of us with fair skin were especially vulnerable. Thank goodness a better, less-harsh product finally came along.

After years of these drenching chores, and in being in the hot Texas sun on a regular basis, Max had skin like leather. Max was about six feet tall, but as lean and wiry as a cheetah. Being somewhat long-waisted, he had super-lean hips and extra-long arms. He didn't appear to be particularly muscular, but one time at the auction when Max was working the center gate, a cow's head got in the way of the swing of the gate and Max had to pull extra-hard on the rope he used to operate the gate. In so doing, muscles that would impress Arnold Schwarzenegger popped up between his elbow and his shoulder under his short-sleeved shirt. No telling how strong he was. His power came not from time spent in a gym but from regular, rigorous physical work.

But it wasn't his rugged appearance that you noticed about Max. It was his super-slow manner of speaking – if he ever finally managed to say anything at all. Yep, Max was mighty quiet. He was a man of very few words. To be sure, he had little to say, but on the rare occasions when he finally did open up, each sentence uttered seemed to take forever. Here's the reason:

It..........would..........be..........impossible..........to..........exaggerate..........how..........slowly..........Max..........talked.

His laughter was similarly subdued. If he became tickled at something, he laughed soundlessly with pursed lips. You were reminded of someone blowing out the candles on a birthday cake. No one would describe Max as effusive or vociferous. His demeanor was one of silence. No one could "out-quiet" Max. His many friends accepted him as he was, and they expected little to no conversation from him, never mind how slowly he talked.

Despite his severe reserve, Max was a solid citizen in every respect and enjoyed spending time with his amigos. Fishing trips to the Pecos River were favored adventures. Several friends of Max have threatened to detail "Maxey" stories in a book. If such a publication ever gets to press, I hope they will include this one:

Back in the days when whitetail deer first made their appearance in the Concho Valley, Max was accompanying Bill Shaw, another Irion County rancher, on some mission. Bro. Shaw, who has a well-deserved reputation for fast driving, was speeding down a remote, lonely lane somewhere in that vast ranch country. As was his habit, Max sat on the passenger side of the truck, as silent as ever. No telling how many miles they had driven without a word exchanged between them.

Finally, Shaw was surprised to hear Max utter a one word, one syllable sentence.

W...O...A...H.

With Max's frugality with words, when finally he did open up, you would inevitably pay close attention. Shaw did. As instructed by Max, Shaw skidded to a stop on the lonely road and turned to face his passenger for more instructions. He couldn't imagine why he had been forcefully ordered to stop.

"What's up, Max?" Shaw implored.

B....A....C....K   U....P. The command was unmistakable. Typically, Max did not repeat himself.

"Why?" Shaw asked excitedly. He could discern no reason for the mission.

Ever so slowly, as was his habit, Max revealed the reason for his statement.

Y...O...N...D...E...R   S...T...A...N...D...S   A   B...I...G   O...L...D   D...E...E...R.

As instructed, Bill put his truck in reverse and using his rearview mirrors to direct his path, succeeded in retreating back down the empty road. Scoped guns are quite common in West Texas ranch vehicles. They can be found in the middle of the seat being pointed toward the floor of the truck, or alternatively, they are readily seen hanging in a gun rack across the rear window of the cab. Max was busy getting that deer rifle out his window. The buck remained immobile.

There he stood in an old, grassy field, about 100 yards from the road. To be sure, he was one impressive whitetail and would be a supreme trophy to almost any deer hunter. When their retreating course finally came to an opening with a decent clear shot, Bill stopped the truck and killed the motor so as not to affect Max's shot from any vibrations.

At this point in the story, it becomes readily apparent that so far, anyway, two crimes are in progress. It is illegal to poach a deer and it is illegal to shoot from a county road. Neither Max nor Shaw hesitated, oblivious to any game laws. Getting that buck on the ground and getting him loaded before someone came along were at the top of their agenda. Max was a good shot, and down the buck went, his lights out for good. He didn't even wiggle.

Hurrying now, the two criminals scampered over the fence and quickly dragged the dead buck toward the truck. Somehow they succeeded in getting him over the fence. Or maybe they shoved him under the fence? The carcass was hefted into the back of Shaw's pickup. With the tailgate closed, and with some old feed sacks thrown over the buck's impressive antlers, which stood well above the sides of Shaw's truck, a casual observer of the vehicle would never suspect that it contained a deer. So far, no one had come along. So far, their crime remained undetected. So far, so good.

All the rigorous work of the last few minutes had winded both men. They clambered back into Shaw's truck and sped away toward their original destination. In all this time, not a word had passed between them. But that was to be expected if you were accompanied by Max Tankersley. Finally, they both caught their breath and settled down for the remainder of the trip.

Max sat there on the passenger side of the vehicle, as stoic as ever. Shaw really didn't expect any conversation out of his companion. But after several miles, Bill was privileged to gain an insight into Max's thinking when Max finally uttered only one, simple, declarative sentence.

Shaw never forgot that bold statement. He has recounted his tale many, many times whenever the subject of Max Tankersley comes up.

What Max finally, finally said that day, fully a half-hour after the fact, was this:

M...A...N, O...H M...A...N - I S...U...R...E D...O G...E...T E...X...C...I...T...E...D W...H...E...N I S...E...E O...N...E O...F T...H...O...S...E B...I...G O...L...D D...E...E...R.

BILL SHAW – LINGUIST

So Bill Shaw tells the story above as if he, himself, is immune to peculiarities regarding the English language. Not so. Shaw is prone to malapropisms from time to time. I only wish I had a list of all of them. Two of his most memorable are these:

Bill was telling me about a mutual acquaintance who found himself in trouble with the law. Shaw said the infraction wasn't all that serious. The guy was only charged with a "misdeemer."

In recent years, Bill has lost considerable weight, but at one point several years ago, he topped-out close to 300 lbs. In those heavy days, he found himself in the hospital with a health issue of some kind or other. I had failed to visit him during his stay.

A few weeks after his dismissal, Shaw revealed some of the details of his experiences over lunch.

"It was the dangdest thing, Skipper," he remembered. "A nurse came by my room every day and weighed me. Day after day, she was there."

I had never heard of such a procedure either. "Gosh, Bill," I asked, "wonder why they do that? That must have been a hassle."

"No, no, no," Shaw assured me. "It wasn't bad at all. In fact, I kind of liked being weighed every day."

"You actually enjoyed being weighed every day?" Good grief. Shaw has always been hard to figure some times, but this was a first. I went on with my thoughts. "What in the world for?"

Shaw didn't quite clear the mystery up, but he did the best he could when he said, "It was that scale they used. It wasn't in 'pounds'. It had great, huge numbers I could see, and I liked looking at that number."

"Oh, yeah?" I wasn't understanding where he was going with this tale. Shaw can be hard to follow.

"It said," Shaw concluded, "that I only weighed 135 Kilo-Meters."

★ ★ ★

Accents

I've said it before. I'll say it again. I hope we Americans never lose our wonderful regional accents. Being an outfitter who accommodates hunters from all corners of the nation, I have enjoyed plenty of strange and odd dialects that can be heard in the English language. Kiddingly I have said that during our hunting season, I'm around so many "foreigners" that I almost lose my own Texas accent. I have been assured there is little danger in this ever happening.

Of course, I am never aware of my own accent. To my ears, I seem to sound just like everyone else. But on those odd and rare occasions when my voice has been recorded, and when I hear myself on tape, my accent is unmistakably pure-dee Texan.

In our own central part of West Texas, there are pockets of super-strong Texas accents. One in particular can be found around Mertzon, in Irion County, just to the west of San Angelo. But strong and unadulterated Texas talk can be found in lots of places. Having been reared in the area, and in traveling the western part of the state all my life, I supposed that I had a workable command of the native lingo and would have no trouble in translating Texan-ese.

During one memorable conversation, I learned that I still had plenty to learn about the Texas dialect.

Back during the days when the cattle business took up most of my time, I was trying to reach Kent Mills on the phone. Kent lived near and worked out of Snyder, Texas, about 100 miles north of San Angelo. Kent's specialty is nutrition for range cattle. He is an expert on the various grasses to be found on West Texas ranches, and he can detail the relative nutritional value of each one of them. To make things even more complicated, this value trends up and down, depending on the season of the year and, of course, moisture availability. It really gets confusing when you consider the calving schedule and re-breeding times for the cow herd and their nutritional demands at the time.

So when the need came to try and blend a ration of supplemental feed for cattle, Kent was the go-to man for expert advice. He would make periodic visits to my ranch to collect grass samples for analysis. We talked often on the phone.

The memorable conversation I mentioned occurred when I once tried to reach Kent at his office in Snyder. A voice with a super-strong Texas accent answered my call. I asked to speak to Kent Mills.

Texas Voice: "I'm sorry. Kent's not here. He's out at the fire."

Me, thinking: Now that's a hell of a way to put it. "Out at the fire?" What the hell is he talking about?

Me, speaking: "Out at the fire? You meant to tell me there is a fire under way at Snyder?"

Texas Voice: "Sure is."

Me, speaking: "Wow. Is it a big one?"

Texas Voice: "I'll say it is. Been going on now three days."

Me, thinking: Good grief. A fire has been burning for three days somewhere around Snyder. Looks like we would have heard something about that on the news.

Me, speaking: "So Kent is helping fight the fire, is he?"

Texas Voice: "Yep, he's been there ever since it started back on Wednesday."

Me, thinking: Mercy. Three days of a fire would cover lots of country. Something of this magnitude would simply have to be on every newscast. This would be a huge, huge deal. Something is amiss.

Me, still thinking, and now befuddled: But wait a minute. On the northern edge of Snyder, I've seen lots of oil fields, tank batteries, and pipelines. Maybe the guy isn't talking about a range fire. Maybe there is an oil field fire of some kind burning out of control near Snyder? That has to be the answer.

Me, speaking: "This fire you are talking about where Kent is helping – is it a range fire, or is he helping fight an oil field fire?"

Texas Voice: "Oh, it's not either one. It's a county fire and livestock show."

I have heard Texans pronounce "fire" to rhyme with "tar". But is it fair to call a "fair" a "fire?"

WIN A FEW

We've all heard the old saying that goes like this:
You win a few, you lose a few, and some get rained out.
I'm not sure my "wins" column is anywhere the length of my "loss" tally. But when the rare victory comes along, it is mighty sweet. And for those of us in West Texas, any event that gets rained out is reason enough for a giant celebration.
This chapter will detail the infrequent times when I could claim victory...

The Big Sting

Unlike some of my more devious friends, I'm not one to pull off giant pranks. But I did once succeed in fooling a whole bunch of people in a magnificent sort of way. It happened when I gave myself a surprise 40th birthday party.
Yes, you read that correctly. I created a surprise party for myself for my 40th birthday. The date of the event was

Tales Galore: And a Whole Lot More

August 27, 1981, the day before my birthday, but the sting took several weeks of plotting and scheming.

To set the scene for the big prank, a review of that time in history is needed. Having gone bald only a couple of years after my college days, I was never able to participate in the long-hair fads which came during the 1970s. Those were the days when short hairstyles for men fell convincingly out of fashion. It seemed as if a majority of males had let their hair grow long enough to cover the tops of their ears. Many men had their ears completely covered. Hair tumbled down over collars, or swooped up in some smart, fashionable style. To my great disgust, even some famous athletes and a sprinkling of cowboys joined the trend. Hippies and other weirdos, of course, wore ponytails.

Being mostly bald, I would have looked ridiculous with any kind of long hairstyle for my limited mane. No doubt my hair follicles would run out of energy before any meaningful length might be realized. Was I jealous of the new look? Well, maybe just a little. The best I could do was to lengthen my sideburns a bit, but that hardly compared with those who had a full mop of hair. I was aghast to learn that some macho friends and acquaintances were even getting their hair "styled" at salons. And the prices they were paying for such foolishness were beyond belief. Thank goodness, one of my closest friends, Dale Bates, still wore a flattop which had been my choice of styles back when I still had hair. I always enjoyed being with Dale in public and didn't feel like an outcast.

Younger men seemed to dominate the long-hair fashions. A surprising number of older guys, say those 40 and older, joined the movement. The fashion changes didn't stop with just the long hair. In an effort to "stay young," men well past their youth were even dressing like college kids. Jimmy Carter, elected president in 1976, wore his hair down over his ears. This trend, in print and in song, was tagged as having gone middle-aged crazy. Jerry Lee Lewis had a popular song with that theme, and there were many others in the same vein.

So at the cusp of becoming middle-age when I turned 40, that seemed like a golden opportunity. I decided to poke some fun at this goofy culture change. With the capable help of my wife, Dorothy, and my mother, I set out to throw a party that would be a giant, unexpected bombshell to every invitee. In planning this surprise party, I planned to fool everyone. I was going to show one and all that I had gone middle-aged crazy. What a hell of a theme for a party. Would anyone who knew me be convinced? Of course not, but I wasn't trying to do anything but pull off a giant trick. If it worked for just a few seconds, all the efforts would be worthwhile.

To get things started, I asked my barber about toupees. Sure enough, he had a catalog in his drawer with a wide variety of styles. I chose one which would fully cover my ears and immediately placed the order. For my charade to be effective, I couldn't use a cheap-o model. That damn wig was mighty expensive but would be powerfully cost-effective if I could pull off this giant ruse.

Next came a proper "costume" for a man who had gone middle-aged crazy. At the mall, I found some skin-tight, designer jeans that no self-respecting cowboy would ever, ever wear. The getup was completed with a silk-looking shirt with a large, open collar. Most of the shirts in my closet were khaki work models, or a couple of ordinary dress shirts. These would never do. My proposed look demanded something flashy. And to top off the new appearance, I needed some jewelry. The only item I wore regularly in this department was my "rubber Rolex" – a black, runner's stop watch which cost about $10.

Dorner Jewelry downtown was delighted to help. I selected a huge necklace which held a genuine shark's tooth. Gaudy, it was, and perfectly accented my disguise. I wasn't about to buy the thing, so I worked out a lease deal with Cheryl Dorner who was amused with my plan and promised to keep quiet.

While all this was going on, Dorothy put together the guest list of about 25 couples of our closest friends. Invitations were sent out, alerting all to be on hand on the appointed evening down at the river park on the ranch. The plan was revealed to the guests. They would spring the big surprise on the unsuspecting Skipper who was turning 40. And for sure, don't leak a word of this event to anyone. The news might get back to the birthday boy and spoil everything.

Sure enough, over the course of the next several days, when I would run into one of the invitees, all remained quite mute and played a convincing part in the scam. The false rumor was that I would be returning from an out-of-town trip late that afternoon. A note would be left for me at our house telling me to come to the river for a small family picnic.

Finally, I needed to hire a young actress. I made some discreet inquiries at Angelo State University and found a willing college performer who would play the part of my "girlfriend." I instructed her to dress a bit provocatively for her co-starring role in my middle-aged crazy production. Heck, we both might win an Oscar for the effort.

About a week before the big event, my new toupee arrived at the barber shop. The color of the thing had been blended to match the tint of my remaining meager locks which circled the bottom of my skull. I was delighted to see that the design was long enough to cover my ears, and it looked plenty authentic with my protruding sideburns which I had let grow a bit for this special occasion.

The barber instructed me on the finer points of wearing a hairpiece. It came with a bit of "stick-um" to hold it in place, but first, he said, I needed to use balls of cotton to apply plenty of rubbing alcohol to remove any oily residue on my scalp. Sure as heck, I didn't want that mop to slip out of place. I listened closely to all his pointers. He put the new creation on my dome and "styled" it to just the effect I had hoped to see. By golly – in his mirror there was a handsome stranger with a full head of hair down over both ears that would be the envy of one and all.

When I got home that afternoon, Dorothy wasn't yet there. I decided I needed a dress rehearsal, so I found a bottle of alcohol and some cotton to see if I could get that toupee to look as good as it had back at the barber shop. It took a while before I was satisfied, but when it finally took on a natural appearance, Dorothy arrived. As she walked into the kitchen, she looked at me and said "Can I help you?" She thought a stranger had invaded her domain. She didn't recognize me at all. After a few seconds of bewilderment followed by her sudden recognition, Dorothy clapped with delight at the surprise. I did too, knowing that my appearance would now be guaranteed to trick all our friends. Hell, Fuzzy. I had just misled Dorothy, hadn't I?

On the day of the party, Dorothy and my mother did a magnificent job of getting the river park ready to go. My buddy, Andy Smith, would be cooking his famous barbecue. Food and drink would be in abundance. The guests had been instructed to be there by 6:30 and don't be late. The birthday boy was expected to arrive at 7 p.m., and the surprise would be sprung on little old me. The guests would all be bringing outrageous cards and gifts for this now middle-aged man. I was to be the butt of many jokes. Little did they know the tables were turning on them even as they plotted their devilment.

For two days, I hid out in my mother's apartment in town so as to be completely out of sight. Remember, I was supposed to be out of town. That gave me plenty of time to get my costume just right. I spent an hour or more just ironing that shirt. I planned to leave the top two buttons open so my shark's tooth necklace would be properly noted there on my hairy chest. (If only I had all that hair on my head, I wouldn't even need that toupee.) So the shirt was ironed to fall open down to about the middle of my chest. The shark's tooth would shine like a spotlight. The designer jeans were ironed, as well. It was a hell of a costume, but until the night of the party, I hadn't yet completed the image with the hairpiece.

On the appointed night, the actress was supposed to come to Mom's apartment at 6:30 for our 30 minute trip to the ranch. To get myself ready, I was dressed in the designer jeans and the necklace. Next, I was going to follow the procedure to properly place the hairpiece. I would leave the shirt for last so as not to get any alcohol on the shiny garment and ruin its looks. I found the liquid and the cotton and began the process of oil removal from my scalp. The featured item – the fake hair – sat over there on its little perch looking jim-dandy. It was 6:15. I was right on time.

Just then, Mom's front door bell rang. What the hell? That actress is 15 minutes early. Damn the luck anyway. I'm not yet ready. But I had to answer the door to let her in. She could just cool her heels in Mom's living room and wait until I got that hair installed in its perfect fashion.

As these thoughts tumbled though my head, I managed to spill some of the alcohol across the top of my head. A generous stream ran down into my right eye.

"Damn, that stuff stings", I thought as I made my way to the door. Blinking violently to subdue the pain in my eye, I opened the door.

But it wasn't the actress. It was a UPS man with a package for Mom. My involuntary blinking wouldn't stop, as I stood there before him shirtless, with that shark tooth necklace around my neck. You should have seen the look on his face. You talk about a "deer in the headlights" stare. His mouth fell open as he took a couple of steps backward and muttered in a breaking voice, "Package for Mrs. Duncan."

He threw that box at me and bolted. Somehow, I managed to catch the thing, even with that blinking eye disrupting my vision.

Finally...finally, I got the toupee the way I wanted it. With my smartly-ironed shirt, I was pleased. I convincingly looked the part of someone who had gone totally, thoroughly middle-aged crazy. The actress arrived right on time, and we two headed for the ranch.

As planned, the party was well under way. Drinks had been served, and everyone was waiting to spring the trap on me. As the actress and I got out of my truck there at the river park (it was a ranch vehicle that none of my amigos recognized as being mine), the guests looked up with mild curiosity to see who the late-arrivers to the party might be. No one recognized me. My "date" and I walked right down in among the group and, as strangers, stood there drawing no interest from anyone.

Maybe it was about 30 seconds, maybe it was a minute. All of a sudden, someone figured out that the tardy arriver was the guest of honor himself. Laughter and hooting echoed through the river park. All conversation ceased. Everyone had to come see the new me, and few could believe their eyes, which were rapidly filling with tears of laughter. Picture after picture was taken. Collectively, they all realized they'd been had. My sting had worked beyond my wildest dreams. I felt as if I'd won the Super Bowl.

But paybacks are hell. Every practical joke requires – no, demands – a reprisal. I should have anticipated this fact.

Even before the meal was served, my profoundly tricked amigos, some of whom wore hairstyles that were now the butt of my joke, gathered themselves into an expeditionary force. Overwhelming me with their superior numbers, they hoisted me by my arms and legs. I was, with great glee, heave-ho'ed into the river. There I flew – designer jeans, silk shirt, shark's tooth, long hair and all. Their blaring threats assured me I had it coming. And I guess I did.

The tragic part of this tale came as I swam back to the dam to climb out of the river. As I exited the water amid all the catcalls and snide remarks, those beautiful locks clinging to my magnificent hair-piece began to give way. Before long, most of my wondrous mane had fallen out.

Just my luck. I noted to the gathering of friends this indisputable fact: It is simply not in the stars for me to ever have a nice head of hair. Heck, I moaned, I can't even keep hair on a toupee. Maybe I wouldn't go middle-aged crazy after all.

The Waiter and the Water in Albuquerque

When it comes to waiters and waitresses, here's the deal: If they do an outstanding job, you hardly notice them, and you leave a tip. If they do a piss-poor job, you really notice them, but you probably leave some kind of a tip anyway and resent having to do so. Seldom is a member of the wait-staff thanked or praised – criticized or rebuked. It ain't necessarily fair, but that's what goes on most of the time. In other words, you rarely "get even with them" on either a positive or negative note.

One time in Albuquerque, I was able to effectively chastise an incompetent waiter. Here's what happened:

Jeri and I had been married about five years. We were in that New Mexico town for a business meeting with Stan Parsons and other members of his consulting group. We were all helping with his "Ranching for Profit" program. Counting the several wives who accompanied our group to a large Mexican restaurant, there were at least a dozen of us in the party. Stan, as a resident of that city, had recommended that popular, out-of-the-way place situated in a large and historic house on the northwestern side of town. It was Saturday night and the joint was super-crowded.

Our group was seated at a large, rectangular table with an equal number of us on both sides, and I found myself at the very end, not a bad place to be in case of fire from that hot New Mexican salsa. For some reason that night, and I honestly don't remember why, I was not drinking beer as was my custom. As drink orders were taken all around, I asked only for water, which finally came with the rest of the drinks. Food orders were placed and conversation was going on all around and across the large table.

But as I said, Mexican food in New Mexico tends to be much hotter than that the milder fare found back home in our Tex-Mex cafes. New Mexican red sauce is plenty hot, but that green stuff they serve will set you free, so to speak. I sampled a bit of both, and it wasn't long until I had drained my glass of water.

The waiter came around asking if any new drinks were needed at the table. Indeed, there were. Another round was called for by someone. I asked for more water. By now, my tongue felt like a branding iron. But the waiter failed to bring water. He seemed, to me anyway, to be focused more on selling drinks than on furnishing free water.

He passed by the table and once again, I begged for more water. I waited. It didn't come. It was time to take matters into my own hands. Someone needed to solve my critical requirement, and if he wasn't going to do anything, I surely could.

Carrying my empty glass back into the large kitchen of that establishment, I found some ice and water. I quickly consumed a couple of helpings to quench my powerful thirst. Just as the fire had burned down to only embers, the manager of the place noticed me back in the kitchen.

"Sir," he demanded. "What are you doing back here in our kitchen?" It was an honest query and deserved an honest answer.

"I'm here to get a drink of water," I replied.

Exasperated now, with the hubbub of activity all around, the managed explained, a bit angrily, that I should ask my waiter for water.

"I already did that," I countered. "Several times. Without results." I was not in the wrong, and I needed to defend my actions.

The manager now grew quite interested in my plight. "I'm so sorry," he responded, as he carefully analyzed the situation. He needed to take action to correct this slight.

"Which waiter," he implored, "is serving your table?"

I looked around the kitchen and just then, our dim-witted server suddenly appeared. "That's him," I pointed. "The one in the white pants."

Assuring me that my problem would be taken care of, the manager walked me out of the forbidden kitchen. But I had won. I had my full glass of water. I made my way back to the table where the conversations continued unabated.

Momentarily, here came the now-chastised waiter. He was carrying a whole pitcher full of water and placed it, without comment, in front of me. His demeanor was that of a dog caught chasing chickens.

With the mighty crowd in the restaurant, the food was a bit slow in finally arriving. More chips and fire-dip – er, ah –

salsa was being consumed by those in our bunch. Could that be their business plan all along to increase sales of drinks? I nibbled away at the basket of tortilla chips and finally could keep the flames at bay with that pitcher of water if I needed to wet my whistle.

After just a bit, my glass of water was either half-full or half-empty, depending on one's optimism or pessimism at the moment. In either case, the waiter spotted this situation and dropped what he was doing to hasten to our table from way across the room. Expertly now, he filled my glass of water from the pitcher sitting right there in front of me. The manager's pep talk had done him a world of good.

More chips, more salsa. Now my water glass was down by only a third. Once again, here came the alert servant to fill it to the brim yet again from the busy pitcher. Dad-gum, this guy just might make something of himself, after all.

The food finally arrived and after getting the proper plates in front of each guest, the waiter once again topped off my water. It was barely below the rim and took only an ounce or so to complete the task.

A golden opportunity suddenly came to me. I'm not normally blessed with good ideas, but this one would be a gem.

I asked if anyone at the table might need water from the pitcher? No one did. I kept my eyes on the waiter closely now, and when he returned to the kitchen for a brief visit, I poured my entire glass of water back into the pitcher.

Once back in the dining room, the alarmed waiter quickly spotted my now-empty glass. He rushed to the scene to fill it from the pitcher. My scheme was beginning to bear fruit.

On another errand to the kitchen, he left the room. Once again I emptied the glass back into the waiting pitcher. And for the second time, he returned to our table in a hell of a hurry to fill my empty glass.

By now, you get the picture, but the poor guy never did catch on. He probably filled my glass a dozen times out of that one pitcher during the rest of our stay. Somehow, it never dawned on him that the pitcher was not running out of water.

So the waiter learned that night to be a better waiter. I am proud to have had a hand in his education.

Reunion Story

With our happy-go-lucky high school class not being up to reunions except every 10 years, our 30th gathering came and went uneventfully. When plans for the 40th gathering were being made by us locals to host our high school brethren, I attended all of the meetings to do my part. Except for the last one, held shortly before the event itself. At that one, in my absence, the scoundrels in attendance at the meeting voted to make me master of ceremonies at the Saturday night banquet. Not one classmate at that infamous meeting would volunteer. Oh gee whiz – what a grim reunion this would be. I'd be worried to death about that burden and couldn't enjoy one minute of the entire weekend.

At most all our reunions, the format generally calls for a Friday night "mixer." This casual event is marked by enthusiastic greetings among folks who probably haven't seen each other in the past 10 years. But since we all grew up together, we have that compelling thread which dominated the first years of our collective lives. There is nothing as enjoyable as connecting with old friends.

And now, four decades after high school, we were all officially "old."

Seeing all the guys at the reunion was as enjoyable as I knew it would be. But greeting all those girls with their enthusiastic hugs was a hoot. I couldn't believe I was being embraced by the many females who had ignored me back in high school. Mercy. Where had all this affection been 40 years ago? These females seemed genuinely glad to see me. Their husbands, if they had them, seemed to accept all this physical groping as a matter of course. I tried to pay some attention to the spouses, but I was mostly interested in their wives' friendliness.

Speaking of wives, I was enjoying myself and oblivious to the fact that my wife, who knew precious few there anyway, had been taking notes of all the gleeful attention being shown to me. It wasn't long before she "suggested" we go home. Just my luck.

I didn't participate in any of the daytime events on Saturday – a golf outing for the men, local tours for the out-of-towners visiting the fabled campus, etc. As was my habit, I went out to the ranch and continued with my current project of building deer blinds. But despite the busy work with my hands, I couldn't get the previous night out of my mind. All those warm, friendly squeezes – wow.

And then, there was that banquet speech to worry about. What the hell would I say?

With such thoughts bearing down, I finally put aside my carpentry tools, and using that giant carpenter's pencil on the back of a feed sack, I composed the following poem to be used that night as I ended the banquet remarks:

At this reunion, it's fun to see everyone,
To get us together again.
Not much has changed. We're still mostly the same.
Just a little older than we were "way back when."

For us guys, what is best, is to hug every girl guest.
Today, it's not even a sin.
These girls, full of charms, wrapped up in our arms —-
In '59, we couldn't even TOUCH them back then.

Each girl in our class is a sweet, little lass.
And they'll return all our hugs 'til we're SORE.
They're no longer afraid, that somehow they'll get laid —
They know we are dangerous no more.

LOSE A FEW

Rob Junell

I don't personally know any famous people. When I was a kid, I got to shake hands with Bob Hope on Guinn Field's baseball diamond where he put on one of the type shows for which he became famous in military circles. Bob spotted me in the crowd wearing my genuine Davy Crockett coonskin cap. He took it off my head and wore it himself for a while, to the great delight of the audience.

Another famous-person encounter came when Tony Churchill invited Jeri and me plus a whole host of his friends to a supper he hosted for his former employee – a pretty darn good cowboy he had hired to help on a large property he managed down in South Texas back

Rob Junell and George Strait

around 1980. The ranch hand? George Strait was his name. After only that one night, most probably George no longer remembers me.

The other famous person at that party actually knows me by name. He is the unforgettable Rob Junell.

Rob is, or rather was, a lawyer by trade. In fact, Rob was a law partner with Guy Choate, son of Wade Choate, one of my good buddies. Both Rob and Guy were associated with one of the most prominent legal firms in town. Interestingly, it was Guy's brother, Vic Choate, who became Rob's all-time best friend. Vic, like his dad, is a cow trader. Exactly why a lawyer and a cow jockey became such fast friends is a mystery. But it's a good match because they are both cut out of the same bolt of cloth – smart as whips and excessively energetic.

Back years ago, we were all runners, and I first got to know Rob at a race. During my running career, I was never blessed with much speed, but because I ran miles and miles each week, I was in pretty good shape. Much better shape than either Vic or Rob, or so I thought. But in San Angelo's legendary "Run in the Sun" 8K one hot day in June, I was within a couple hundred yards of the finish line. Rob Junell ran past me as if I were hobbled. Having an opponent pass you so close to the finish line is hard on your ego. It's oh so much better if you pass them.

Come to find out, Rob had played both football and baseball for Texas Tech, the same college I had attended. Being a few years younger, Rob's athletic accomplishments had escaped my notice. But I quickly learned the facts. Talk about a competitor. There was no way I could have beaten him, speed or no speed – training or no training. Rob's passion is winning.

As I got to know Rob better, I continually marveled at his lightning-quick mind. No doubt it was this native intelligence that made him a formidable competitor, no matter the endeavor. But even so, his outgoing personality won him many, many friends. I cannot think of anyone who does not love Rob Junell. He is an extrovert if there ever was one, and within five minutes of entering a crowded room, he will have spoken to everyone by name.

Vic and Rob soon grew tired of running as they conquered even more sports. Now, Guy Choate was involved, too. They all took up team roping and got pretty darn good at that cowboy pastime. Finally, the collection of horsemen got wholeheartedly into polo. They had the flat saddles, the mallets and the helmets to become ferocious competitors in yet another sport. Keen rivalry sprinkled with fun ruled their games.

Somewhere along the line, Rob the lawyer got into politics. Vic, of course, was tabbed to be his campaign manager. What a bold stroke of genius. Few politicians have ever considered the wisdom of having a cow trader on their team. One's mind boggles at the possibilities.

Running as a Democrat in our heavily Republican West Texas, Rob easily won the race for state representative to the Texas Legislature. I paid little attention to state government back then, but it wasn't long before Rob succeeded in gaining the chairmanship of the appropriations committee. Deciding how the state will spend its money is truly one of the most powerful positions in Austin. Rob, ever the master opportunist, made the most of it for his district.

He was a conservative Democrat, to be sure, skillfully working closely with the tight-fisted Republicans. But as politicians are prone to do, Rob took care of his constituents back home. If it wasn't for Rob, the Houston Harte Expressway running through the heart of San Angelo would still be unfinished. We had driven on frontage roads for years as the dusty would-be freeway just sat there covered with weeds. He also saved our local railroad. His list of accomplishments while in office would fill a book. And as a Democrat, he worked hand-in-hand with our Republican governor at the time, George W. Bush. They were, and still are, fast friends.

So when Mr. Bush became President of the United States, and when it came time to find a federal judge for West Texas, guess who got the nomination? Yep, Rob Junell. By then, Rob had retired from the Legislature and had returned to the practice of law.

For several years, our First Presbyterian Church had been hosting a men's Bible study on Wednesday morning. The gathering was the creation of then-pastor Dale DePue. Over time, there were 15 to 20 attendees, jam-packed into a small conference room. Rob and I were regular attendees.

This same group has been together for over 25 years and now counts pert-near 50 or 60 men as faithful members. Thankfully, the church now allows us to use a much larger room. Interestingly enough, our current inimitable leader, Ross Dawkins, and probably a majority of each week's students, aren't even members of that church. But that's another story.

Back in the days when we were crammed into that small conference room, and as the meeting concluded one Wednesday morning, everyone dispersed outside for brief chats before heading off to the day's adventures. It just so happened that I fell in beside Rob Junell as we walked to our cars lined up there on that tall curb on Irving Street. There were three or four other groups, each with three or four similar conversationalists scattered nearby.

Not being up to date on Rob's situation, I asked him this question:

"Rob," I wondered as we moved toward the street, "I hear you have been nominated to be a federal judge by President Bush. But nothing has been in the news lately. What's going on? What is happening to the deal? Are you ever going to become a federal judge?"

Rob began his reply in a most interesting manner. "Everything just now is very intense, Skipper. The FBI is doing a background check on me. I've never seen anything quite like it after all my years in government. Everything about that entire process is simply astonishing. You wouldn't believe it."

Oh boy. This was going to be some fascinating news. I didn't want to miss a word of it.

We'd arrived at the curb. As I reached to put my Bible on the hood of my truck, still totally mesmerized by Rob's story and his continued monologue, I turned my back to the street. But I misjudged the location of the curb. I stepped backwards off the thing right out into space. One of my typical, clumsy moves. A crash landing was the only predictable outcome.

Remember now, I claimed earlier that Rob is a very, very quick thinker. Here's proof.

In the blink of an eye, he seized this golden opportunity, even as I was just beginning that fall. How the hell he came up with this statement at warp speed, I'll never know.

He hollered in a super-loud voice:

"AND DON'T YOU EVER SAY THAT TO ME AGAIN, SKIPPER DUNCAN, OR I'LL HIT YOU AGAIN."

He got the entire sentence out of his mouth before I summarily hit the street on my butt.

With that quick mind of his, he knew the several nearby groups from the Bible study would turn in unison to see me crash onto the pavement.

No one who witnessed my fall that morning ever admitted it, but they were all probably thinking the same thing: Duncan needs to be paying closer attention in Bible study. Maybe he will learn to speak to Rob in a more Christian-like manner.

Tales Galore: And a Whole Lot More

Blake Duncan – Young Farmer

The summer before my son Blake turned 14, I resolved to instill responsibility and hard work into his character. It would be good for him. His boyhood was ending. He was on the cusp of becoming a young man. He should play less and work more. He needed accountability training. Work is defined as doing something that needs to be done even if you'd rather be doing something else. If it's fun, it isn't work. Blessed are those whose work is fun.

To guide Blake along into becoming a productive member of society, I thought I had the perfect solution. Plowing wheat stubble would be educational for him. That is a traditional summer task on Texas farms and ranches. Many, many lessons can be instilled while astride a tractor. It is the perfect environment for thinking. You can dwell of life's mysteries and all that.

No, I wasn't trying to get myself out of this boring task. Well – er, umm – maybe just a little.

One of the biggest mistakes I ever made was trying to save money by purchasing a tractor without a cab. Over the years, my sitting all day on that behemoth took its toll. It was dusty (which contributed to my lung problems); it was loud (which has certainly affected my hearing); it was sunny (which finally caused a skin cancer on my lip). But all this wisdom didn't come until after the damage had already been done. A cab-less tractor is injurious to your health. One of these days, some benevolent bureaucrat in the Department of Agriculture will address this problem. Or at the very least, there will be a warning label if they can find a new place to stick one.

Speaking of dust, there is this important point to consider. With almost any endeavor you can think of, a tailwind is desirable. Not so with plowing. A modest wind from your backside, if it is blowing in the exact direction of your path, envelops you in a cloud of dust. With a dastardly tailwind, many times I was forced to come to a complete halt just to see where I was headed once the dust cleared. When you are plowing, a headwind is your friend. If you are plowing a rectangular field at right angles, at some point during your travels, you will be dealing with a tailwind.

With Blake being 13 years old at the time, the purpose of the tractor and plow wasn't just turning dirt upside down. The larger role of the process was to help instill a good work ethic in my young son. For that magnificent purpose, the machine would be of incredible value, cab or no cab.

Admittedly, just like young Blake, I hated plowing. Hours and hours of boredom going round and round a field is a mighty grim way to spend your day. I would sing every song I knew, and I know a bunch of them. As I remember the details, that 100-acre field could be entirely plowed in about 25 hours. Yes, our equipment in those days was infinitely faster than the old "Popping Johnnies." Or going even further back – horse-drawn plows. We were zipping along working maybe four acres each hour. Big tractors today are capable of 10 times that – maybe more.

But here's the deal: 10 hours of plowing wouldn't even be half of it. Yet – 10 hours traveling in a car would get you from San Angelo to Albuquerque or to Little Rock or to Vicksburg, Mississippi. After 10 hours on that tractor, I was never out of sight of my house. The scenery never changed.

With the disc plow being used at the time, the first lap around the outside perimeter of the 100 acres took almost an hour. The second lap took a brief few seconds less, and so on. Each succeeding wrap might be just a wee-wee bit faster if you timed it. But it seemed to take forever before you felt as if you were finally making any noticeable progress. And, here's a truism: There are no shortcuts. You sorely want to use a faster gear on the tractor. But that little trick doesn't bring the RPM meter up to the correct point. You are abusing the tractor by trying to gain speed in this manner. So you are stuck in a gear that is so, so slow. There is no other option.

It is just a given – you have to sit for hours and hours, toiling away in the hot sun to get that land plowed. For us cowboy types – which certainly described both Blake and me – plowing was the most hated job on the ranch. Working livestock was infinitely better. Real farmers, come to find out, actually enjoy plowing, or at least they have told me they do. I could never understand why.

With these thoughts in mind, I had no doubt that this work would be instructive for young Blake. He would learn that any task can finally be completed if you stick to it. You gotta keep that tractor rolling. That's the secret.

Of course when Blake plowed and when every lap of the field brought him back in front of our house, he would find some pretext to stop. He had to go to the bathroom. He was thirsty. He was hungry. He needed a better hat. He never ran out of excuses to visit the house, and with that tractor sitting out there with the motor idling waiting for his return, the plowing was not getting done.

I had been through this battle with Blake often. Keeping him on that tractor, come what may, was a challenge if there ever was one. If nothing else, he was getting quite adept at creative excuses.

BLAKE DUNCAN

I got him started early one July morning. The tractor was full of fuel with everything set to go. The first lap or two around the field the previous afternoon had set the pattern and it was up to him to keep laying down the ribbons of plowed ground to the inside of the huge rectangle. Away he went as I wondered what new excuse he would concoct for stopping once he arrived back in front of the house on that first loop. Meanwhile, I had some livestock to check from horseback. I saddled up, loaded the pony in the trailer for the trip to the far side of the ranch and hoped for the best.

My task, whatever it was, took longer than I had anticipated. It was pert-near three hours before I finally returned to the headquarters. But with my first glance at the field, I was heartened to see that, indeed, there was that tractor doing its duty way down yonder in the far end by the Kelly fence. A cloud of dust boiled up behind the slow-moving machinery. And in looking at the progress that had been made during my absence, well goodness-sakes-alive – numerous wraps had been made and a visible advancement was clearly evident.

I made my way to the horse corral in a good mood. As I unsaddled, I kept mulling over the same pleasant topic. Similar to the progress gained in plowing that field, I was making headway – albeit slowly but surely – with raising my son to be an energetic worker. Maybe the boy would learn responsibility and hard work after all. Why, just look at that tractor out there in that field, even with the day getting hotter and hotter. It was still going round and around. I gave the horse a bucket of oats as thanks for his morning's work and headed to the house for a cool drink of water for myself, badly needed by this time of day. I saw the tractor pass by the front of the house without stopping. Yes sir, that boy was going to amount to something after all. Was I proud of him? Or proud of myself for being such an exemplary father?

Imagine my surprise as I walked into the house to find Blake, relaxing with his shoes off and sitting on the couch, watching television. Talk about dumfounded. I was momentarily speechless. The recent evidence I had seen with my own eyes just didn't add up. The tractor was making its laps, but the supposed driver of the tractor was unmistakably right there in the house. Solving this riddle suddenly became much more important than that drink of water.

"Good grief, Blake," I protested. "What in the world are you doing in the house? What is that tractor doing out there in the field? Who is driving the thing? What is the meaning of all this?"

Rather than displaying an attitude of sheepish guilt as I expected, Blake appeared smug and proud. Condescendingly, he got quickly to the point of his grand achievement.

"Pop," he began assuredly, "you are paying me two dollars an hour to plow. Isn't that correct?"

I nodded an affirmation, trying to follow his logic.

"Well," he went on cockily, "I called John Hofmann right after you left with the horse. His mother brought him out here. I'm paying him a dollar an hour to plow and he thinks it's a great deal. So do I.

I could find another friend if we had a second tractor, too. Then I could really make some money."

In all the great history of the world, wheeler-dealers have always been more successful than common laborers. So I suppose I should have been proud of his creativeness. Without a doubt, I was rearing a horse trader. As it's turned out over the years, he has proven to be pretty good at deal-making. That plowing chore taught him a lesson all right. It just wasn't the one I had intended.

At least that field was getting plowed. And at least it wasn't me on that tractor.

Some Get Rained Out

West Texas is normally extra dry. Except when it is extra wet. Yeah, there may be some in-between times, but not often. It's best to expect either one or the other. Come to think of it, there ain't much in-between around here. Sadly, it seems as if the dry days outnumber the wet ones by a substantial margin.

The weather records state that a typical year in San Angelo will see about 20 inches of rain. But the annual accumulation varies from a low of 8-9 inches during a terrible drought to maybe as high as 40 inches during a super-wet year. This is one heck of a wild swing. Over the decades, annual totals are calculated into an "average," a figure which is virtually meaningless. Realistically, ours is a boom or bust environment.

I once talked to a cattleman who ranched up north somewhere – maybe it was Nebraska. He was telling me how much hay they put up for their cows, and I don't recall the exact figures but it was something like 1,000 big, square bales. I asked him how much hay they would produce in an extra-good year. He remembered one special time when they harvested 1,200 bales. When I asked about the worst year they ever had, he bemoaned the fact that one particularly horrible year they put up only 800 bales.

As a lifelong West Texan listening to his story, I marveled at the reliability of his hay production. It sounded great to me. Around our area, we have plenty of years when our hay production might be zero bales, or close enough to zero to make a harvest not even worthwhile. But in an extra-good year, a farm with a 1000 bale average might make 3,000 bales. So the good times around here are really, really good and the dry years are way worse than bad.

The rancher trying to determine a proper stocking rate for his livestock has an impossible challenge. There are years when having 10% of a normal number on his ranch is too many. During the infrequent wet times, there is not enough money in the World Bank to buy the livestock you could run. Things are complicated enough as they are, but not knowing the amount of future rainfall is the eternal mystery. If you just knew when rain would come and how much might accumulate, it would certainly help your planning. But that is impossible, so livestock owners struggle along as best they can.

In this regard, ranchers are rarely "properly" stocked. At any given time, they have either too much livestock or too little livestock. And even if they just happened, by chance, to be perfectly stocked at any one time, that condition could change within a month. Thirty days later they would be over or under the magic number.

It was once claimed that Tom Green County had more miles of flowing streams than any county in Texas. I don't think we could earn that title anymore. But our area does have lots or rivers and draws which drain a substantial expanse of West Texas. Extra-wet spells have sometimes produced horrendous floods.

Our county seat back before 1882 was Ben Ficklin, a small town on the South Concho River about 5 miles south of what is now San Angelo which sits on the northern bank of the North Concho River. The confluence of the two streams is on the eastern edge of the city. In September of that year, a huge flood obliterated Ben Ficklin taking 65 lives and most of that town's buildings in the process. Following that disaster, the county seat was moved to San Angelo, but future flooding still came from time to time. In 1936, a two-week wet spell brought flood after flood not only on the North Concho but all the area rivers. Large parts of downtown San Angelo were under water.

Interestingly enough, major floods have hit West Texas during dry times. In 1954, right smack in the heart of the legendary seven-year drought of the 1950s, waters in the Pecos River and all the major draws in Crockett County to our southwest reached historic levels never matched since. A flood in the midst of a devastating drought seems to be an anomaly. Indeed, that event was tragically misunderstood at the time as the end of the dry weather. Livestock folks held on, unwisely as it turns out, by trying to feed their way through to better times. But the famous drought had three more years to go.

West Texans rarely complain about wet weather or floods. In fact, a rainy spell around here puts everyone into an extraordinarily good mood. Rain gauge levels will be compared proudly and endlessly in coffee shops and cafes. Woe to the poor guy who makes the first claim. Almost immediately, some reporter will top his reading only to be displaced moments later by another gauge-reader. It isn't exactly a contest, but rain gauge comparisons in West Texas are taken to majestic levels.

I remember my dad looking at rain gauges at the ranch. He would lift the tube to eye level, peering carefully through his bifocals, and then tip the thing back toward himself to amplify the level of the liquid in the tube. He could inflate a half-inch rain total to ¾-inch easily and without remorse.

Rainy spells don't last forever, but dry times seem to have no end. As it begins to get dry in town, alarm begins to mount. When a drought begins to really tighten its grip, many church marquees will urge everyone to "Pray for Rain." And of course, we always do. One of the most memorable preachers in town, Nathaniel Hankins at the First United Methodist Church, when making his weekly plea for rain, would invariably hoist an umbrella (unopened, of course) to the delight of the congregation as he began his appeal.

The famous prayer for rain written by W.L. White of Emporia, Kansas, during the heart of the Dust Bowl days in 1935 starts with a plea not for just a shower but for a real deluge. For the next several paragraphs, the author details a litany of his wishes from sheets of rain on a tin roof to pigs and chickens floating down the river. When it gets really, really dry in West Texas, that memorable piece is dusted off and brought back into service.

Every so often during a particularly wet spell, a West Texas farmer will, almost ashamedly and under his breath, bemoan the rain because he cannot get into his fields to plant or to harvest. Such talk is heard only from tillers of the soil. It is clearly blasphemous to ranchers. Livestock people never get enough rain and will always be eager to get more and more. This will be true even if they have scores of water gaps to repair in their fences from the flooding. If a rancher gets stuck in one of his pastures, he will whistle a tune during his hike back to headquarters while he is checking the clouds hoping for more rain.

In those rare times around here when it gets really, really wet, I am guilty of thinking that finally, things are back to normal. I forget how dry it can get. Conversely, when the dust blows day after day in 100-degree weather, and we get nary a drop for months on end, I forget how wet it can get.

One particularly wet fall it had been raining for two months. It was some year back in the late '60s or early '70s. I was a member of the committee which helped with the big roping fiesta weekend, held in those days on the first weekend in November. The big roping contest by then was an institution. The weekend brought plenty of people to San Angelo – it was impossible to find a motel room.

The big draw for the event was the matched calf roping. Every year, our favorite West Texas roper, Jim Bob Altizer, would compete against the previous year's PRCA champion on 12 head of calves each. You talk about exciting – it was the Super Bowl of calf roping. And if somehow you could confiscate all the money bet on the contest, you could almost pay off the national debt (back in those long-ago days anyway.)

The contest was held, rain or shine, and drew probably 5,000 spectators with substantial others on hand for standing-room-only privileges. And with the wet fall under way, everyone coming would be in extra-good moods. Nothing cheers a Texan like wet weather. During the preceding two months, maybe 15 inches of rain had come.

So it was Friday afternoon, the day before the big event. All of us committee members were on hand making preparations. And it was raining. The roping arena looked like a pond. You could see small patches of soil here and there among the sheets of water, but not many. And the rain continued to fall. You couldn't call it a drizzle. It was an honest-to-goodness rain.

The star of the show, Jim Bob Altizer was there at the arena fence along with his brother-in-law, Bud Smith. Both lived and ranched near Del Rio, Texas, just 150-plus miles south, and still firmly in West Texas. Jim Bob had won the title of World Champion Calf Roper in 1959, but after that feat, he devoted most of his time to ranching. He competed at only a few select rodeos each year.

Bud Smith was another good roper who always stayed pretty close to home. Bud would help his kinsman during the match contest in whatever capacity that was needed.

Although both Jim Bob and Bud were highly skilled ropers, they were mainly ranchers at heart. In fact, their substantial ranching interests took up way too much time for extensive rodeoing. Both had livestock aplenty which demanded most all their attention.

So there we all stood on that afternoon before the big event. Even if the sun came out that very minute, it was a cinch that the ground would still be a loblolly during the following afternoon's contest. And the forecast held no promise of sunshine. All of us were wearing slickers and rubber boots. Rain dripped steadily off everyone's cowboy hat. There was no conversation. What could be said? The roping would be held, come what may. We would all be slopping around in boot-top-muck. Silent gloom prevailed.

Finally, after an inordinate time of the misery, a voice was heard. It was Bud Smith. Out of nowhere, he uttered a simple, declarative sentence. He said matter-of-factly:

"I wish it would quit raining."

More silence. Everyone had heard him, but no response came from the assembled group.

Bud then followed that astounding declaration with another memorable statement which turned out to be a virtual apology to his companions.

"There. I said it. I wish it would quit raining. I meant every word of it, too."

In all his born days, and all the days yet to follow in his life, that was the only time he ever uttered those immortal words. Ranchers around here just never say such things.

DO-OVERS

As life unfolds and daily decisions are made, we all do the best we can with what we have at the time. No one ever sets out purposely to make an incorrect decision. Oh sure, some of our choices turn out to be goofy or ill-conceived. When that happens, we have to live with the consequences.

One of my favorite sayings is "in the fullness of time." If we knew then what we know now, a different decision would have been made, no doubt. In the fullness of time, those things once obscured come more sharply into focus.

My favorite modern device is the "delete" key. Too bad it only works on computers.

But for some events, you really wish there were do-overs. Oh, if that action could simply be erased and, oh, if we could just start over, knowing what we now know – in the fullness of time.

I've had many such experiences. I will now recount a few of them in hopes that these stories will prevent others from similar disasters.

A Dalmatian on the Bed

After Dorothy and I had lived in Lubbock for a year or so while we were attending Texas Tech, we finally moved west of the city to a small town, Carlisle, where we found a house with a small stable for my horse. I was just getting into roping calves at the time, and everyone knows you can't rope calves without a horse.

Dorothy, being the daughter of a rancher at Rocksprings, Texas, was well acquainted with horses and animals of all kinds. Living on that small acreage west of Lubbock, it wasn't long until we had acquired a Dalmatian dog, Peggy, and a tabby cat we called "Top Cat," named after a cartoon character on television. Neither pet earned its keep. I once found a mouse in my barrel of oats and put Top Cat in with him to (a) give him a free meal and (b) rid my oats of mouse droppings. Top Cat fell asleep while the mouse scampered about looking for an exit.

Peggy, the dog, had no specific job but enjoyed house privileges anyway. I didn't really mind keeping a canine in the house, having been reared in a home where a dog had always been part of our family. But what aggravated my annoyance was Peggy's sneaky habit of sleeping on our bed, uninvited to be sure.

Deep in the night, she would creep onto the foot of the bed and curl up on the soft covers. Never mind that she had her own adequate bed elsewhere. Oh, no. She insisted on sleeping on our bed, making a huge lump that left little room for my feet to wiggle. Kind of like wearing tight boots all night long.

Whenever I was aroused from my slumber, I would invariably shoo her off the bed. But that never worked for long. If I woke up some time later, there would be that giant anvil-like lump at the foot of the bed.

No matter how many admonitions and threats and cussing's, Peggy was learning no lesson in the matter. Her habit was impossible to break. It was time for drastic action.

Late one night, I "fell awake." There, as usual, was Peggy in the bed. Sometimes we humans do our best thinking in the middle of the night. Revenge was on my mind. I determined then and there that I would teach that dog a lesson she'd never forget. My plan was to slowly move both my feet right up next to the sleeping dog and, doubling my knees up for more power, I would forcefully push her off the bed. What a powerful message that would be. I lay there a few minutes, enjoying the thought. It was a masterful plan. She would never forget it. Ever so slowly, I moved my feet into position. Simultaneously, I drew up both knees for my power move.

Finally, with all the strength I could muster, I pushed hard with both feet and yelled at the top of my voice: "TAKE THAT, YOU HUSSY." Bed covers flew in all directions.

The commotion aroused the sleeping Peggy, slumbering contentedly there on her pallet in the corner of the room. My feet had been against the small of Dorothy's back. She hit the floor on her side of the bed, bewildered beyond belief, before she started wailing and crying.

You talk about apologies. I was so full of them, not only the remainder of that night, but for days and days thereafter. It's a wonder that I wasn't consigned to sleeping on Peggy's bed for the rest of the year.

Yep, a do-over would have saved much anguish if I only had one to play at the time. Did this tragic event contribute to our divorce twenty-some years later? Could be. Having a bit of experience with an abusive husband, Dorothy ultimately gained her credentials as a family counselor.

Tales Galore: And a Whole Lot More

Handsome Les and Carol Santry

I failed to attend my high school's class reunion on the 10th anniversary of our graduation. Reason: rodeoing was more important, and I was entered in the calf roping at the Fourth of July event at Pecos. By the time the 20th-anniversary reunion rolled around, all that roping foolishness was out of my system. I was eager to see my classmates after those many years. Indeed, it was a grand gathering.

During the ensuing two decades since graduation, one of the girls in our group, Carol Santry, had unfortunately gone blind. In fact, she had been sightless for many years by then, but her uplifting spirit and gracious good humor were, and still are, inspirations to one and all. That blindness has slowed her not one bit. Everyone loves Carol, and she loves everyone in turn. She is one special lady.

But it is incredible how those unfortunate victims afflicted with the loss of one particular sense will compensate by gaining additional skills with their remaining faculties. Carol, blind though she is, intuitively recognizes many things that go right over my head. Her perceptions are uncanny and almost always right on target.

Case in point: At that reunion, I was schmoozing with lots of folks when up walks "Les" (his name has been changed for reasons that will become obvious shortly). Unlike the rest of us whose physical appearance had declined during the ensuing 20 years, Les now looked like a movie star. Back in high school, his appearance was most ordinary. He hadn't won "Most Handsome" to get his photo in our yearbook, but he would have easily claimed the honor at this reunion if a vote had been held. I couldn't believe my eyes. He was incredibly attractive and could have been a model for catalogs.

Give credit where credit is due – that's my motto. And so I congratulated Les on his appearance. Slim, trim, perfect hair and complexion. I went on and on, genuinely, sincerely fascinated as I told him how impressed I was with his good looks. Finally he wandered off, no doubt basking in all my effusive praise.

Carol Santry, sitting nearby at the time, had heard the whole thing.

She whispered: "Skipper. Come here."

When someone has spoken so softly, you naturally assume they want to speak confidentially. She did.

I found a nearby chair and pulled it up close for privacy. She was unusually serious, with a scowl on her face.

"Skipper," ordered Carol in her muted, deep voice. "You should be careful bragging on Les like that." She was quite emphatic.

"Why? I was just trying to be nice." I saw nothing wrong with anything I had said.

"Skipper – Les is gay. He probably thinks you are making a pass at him." Oooowwwwww. Now how the hell did she know that?

Thankfully, I didn't see any more of Les later on. Maybe because I kept avoiding him on purpose after Carol's admonition. A do-over would have saved me much anguish. I never should have bragged on ol' Les like that.

Boy's Town Tour

After completing our studies at Texas Tech, my wife, Dorothy, and I moved home to the family ranch. She found a teaching job in town, and I busied myself with ranch work. Like so many others in the same boat, we had a very small budget for vacations or entertainment. Just before school was to start and she was to begin her new teaching job, we decided to go to the bullfights in Via Acuna, across from Del Rio, situated about 165 miles south of home.

Accompanying us on the trip were some dear friends. Like us, they were a young married couple just starting out. In an effort to maintain their friendship and good will, they shall remain anonymous since their identity is not important to the punch line of the story anyway. Besides, they would never forgive me for including their names in a book such as this one.

In those early 1960s, bullfights were held a few times a year in Acuna. Yes, they were brutal and somewhat bloody, but heck, so is today's NFL football. The entertainment wasn't limited to just the bullring. Lots and lots of people came to enjoy the food and drink to be found in that border city, and prices were surprisingly cheap, comparatively speaking. So it was a great mini-vacation for those on a tight budget. Colorful curio shops lined the main drag of the Mexican city where cheap trinkets and paintings on velvet could be admired. Some even bought the things. A bullfight weekend drew hundreds of people, and it was common to run into numerous friends and acquaintances. The entire event produced a party atmosphere all around and frankly, the bullfights themselves were not the main entertainment.

On our second and final afternoon in Acuna, the two young wives came up with a big idea. They wanted to see "Boy's Town." Right then and there, I should have put my foot down with an unequivocal "NO."

For those unfamiliar with the term, "Boy's Town" was the fabled area of Acuna where the brothels and vulgar bars were concentrated. Most of the border towns on the Mexican side had such places. This den of sin was situated some distance from the middle of town where the better restaurants, the bars, the curio shops and the bullring were situated. You had to make a concerted effort to find the place. Casual visitors to Acuna would be unlikely to stumble into Boy's Town while wandering the city.

Both wives had heard of Boy's Town. Most every young person had. Back in those days, the super-cheap and easy sex to be found across the border drew visitors from all over Texas. Many teenaged boys, whether they had been there or not, dreamed of Acuna in their sleep. The Victorian-like age of the 1950s and early '60s was still in full force, so a young man's best chance of finding an outlet for his lust was in Boy's Town. The wild and crazy hippy days with the free love and sex were still to come. One has to wonder if this craze, when it came, caused an economic depression in all the Boy's Towns up and down the border.

So the two properly-raised girls, now blushing young brides, wanted to see Boy's Town. Not to get out and wander around, you understand – just see the place. A quick drive-through, that's all. A picture is worth a thousand words – all their questions would be answered. No stopping, no parking. What could that hurt? What could go wrong?

My alarm bells were ringing off the wall. It was NOT the thing to do. I had forebodings of bad results. My friend, who himself had never seen the place, was mildly curious as well, but he was nowhere nearly as insistent as those two young wives. Everyone knows how persuasive women can be when they set their mind to something. I continued to harbor a strong premonition that something would go terribly wrong. I was totally against the idea.

After the barrage of their constant badgering, and just to put the issue to rest, I finally agreed to a quick tour late in the afternoon. Directions to the place weren't hard to come by, and the four of us piled into my friend's car. He had a state-of-the-art 1962 Chevy two-door hardtop. (What would that vehicle be worth today?) The girls sat in the back. My friend drove. I sat in the front passenger seat with a sense of impending doom beginning to overwhelm me.

When we arrived at the fabled location, it was about 6 p.m. Ribald activity on the streets wouldn't commence until later, but the working girls were just beginning to come out to enjoy the cool of the evening before getting serious about earning some money. They were dressed up in the best, most suggestive garments they owned. With plenty of makeup and wild hair-dos, their goal, of course, was to try to attract as much attention as possible.

Boy's Town wasn't very large. As you entered, the main road forked to go a block or two with bars lining both sides of the street, loud music blaring all around. Take your pick. There was plenty of Mexican music, but some of the joints featured either rock 'n' roll or country music of the day. My friend was driving as slowly as he could with all the windows in that car rolled down to provide better viewing. The two girls in the back seat were looking right and left, side to side, as quickly as possible so as not to miss a thing. They ooohed and aaahed upon seeing several outrageously flashy garments worn by the main attractants of the place.

So far, so good. We were almost halfway done.

We made a left turn to go a block before making another left turn to put us back on the other main drag with still more loud bars. That route would take us back to that fork in the road and, hopefully, out of there for good. I could hardly wait. The same female scenery covered this last leg of the journey. No telling how many girls worked in the area.

Streets in Boy's Town are mighty narrow. Our slow progress almost had us to the end of the journey. But there on my side of the car, standing right on the curb, was a "girl of the night." She had spotted us coming toward her, moving slowly.

There is no doubt that women of that profession have well-developed skills in reading people and situations. In studying our approaching car, with the two males in the front, and the two goggle-eyed young gringo women in the rear seat, she quickly analyzed the entire situation. Because our path would take us within inches of her, all of us in the car were anticipating this close encounter. We would be close enough for her to touch the car if she wanted. We all gawked, transfixed by the sight. Equally hard, she stared back at us, making eye contact with everyone in the car. Just as we pulled alongside of her, our pace was as slow as a snail, and with that window down for all to hear, the calamity I knew was coming crashed down upon me like an avalanche.

Looking me right in the eye, that painted lady said in her Spanish accent, but with perfectly understandable English:

"Hey, cowboy. Remember me?"

I wanted to melt down and disappear into the carpet in that car.

From then on, not only for the rest of that trip, but for years thereafter, if my friend or his wife ever really wanted to get my goat, all they had to utter was that now infamous line:

"Hey, cowboy. Remember me?"

Remember, hell. No one in the car ever forgot it.

I started out by talking about "do-overs." If only I had not agreed to that tour of Boy's Town.

Tales Galore: And a Whole Lot More

Summary: Do-Overs

It has been said that every person you encounter is someway your superior. No doubt, this is a true fact. If you keep your antennae up, you can gain great wisdom from almost anybody.

My uncle, Ball Duncan, had a dairy farm at Knickerbocker, about 20 miles southwest of San Angelo. In fact, that acreage was the original home place of the Duncan family. Periodically, I would visit Uncle Ball and Aunt Lucille. Ball was quite a character and many tales could be told about him. I always enjoyed our time together.

This story, related to do-overs, however, is about one of Uncle Ball's employees. Willie worked around the dairy at various odd jobs. Willie wasn't entrusted to milk the cows for one very good reason – he was mentally impaired. His condition wasn't easily hidden. In just a brief conversation with Willy, it became abundantly clear that he was not quite right. For one thing, his speech was somewhat slurred and a conversation with him was disjointed and confusing. I never quite knew what he was talking about.

Despite his handicap, he was good at what he did. There is always something to do around a dairy – cleaning up this, repairing that, digging there, unloading here. He was a willing worker and proved to be a valuable assistant for Uncle Ball who was, by then, getting too old for the unending heavy work demanded by a dairy.

On one memorable visit to the dairy, while I was waiting for Uncle Ball to finish consulting with the man who actually milked the cows, I found Willie at his small house. It was late in the afternoon. The milking was done, the hay had been put in the mangers and the day was almost over. I asked Willie about things, what he'd been doing, etc. Willie had few visitors and he was eager to find someone to hear stories about his adventures of the day. I pride myself on being a good listener and asker of questions. Willie was going on and on, and I understood only about half of what he said.

About that time, walking across the cow lot there in front of Willie's house was an armadillo. He (she?) was poking along, nose to the ground, as that species is prone to do, in a search for edible morsels of grubs or worms or roots of some kind. Willie spotted the critter immediately and gave out a whoop of joy.

"Oh boy," he hollered, "there goes my supper." I had heard that armadillos are edible, but I knew few people who ever ate them. Willie, apparently, was an armadillo gourmet. It was manna from heaven, judging by the look on his face. Having no gun or weapon of any kind, Willie set out to capture the potential meal with his hands.

It is only mildly difficult to catch an armadillo. Just to see if I could do it, I have been successful several times. The trick is this: While they are moving, you can move closer to them. When they stop periodically (for whatever reason that causes an armadillo to halt his progress), you, too, must immediately halt. They can neither hear nor see very well, so if you are immobile, they probably won't detect your presence. When they begin to move again, you can too, thereby closing the distance to your quarry.

If you are successful in playing this game, you can get right smack on top of the armadillo, and he will never realize you are there. Then, it comes time for the capture. The trick is to grab the quarry by the tail, which, up close to their body, is about the size of the small end of a baseball bat. Don't seize the end of their tail. It's not large enough for an adequate hold. The only thing to remember at this point is this: You simply, positively MUST hang on to that tail for all you are worth.

For about 10 or 15 seconds, the captured animal will, with surprising strength, roll and twist and torque himself every which way. For a few moments there, you will imagine that your wrist might break. But when this brief flurry of struggle is over, the captured critter will hang there immobile, docile as can be. If you don't have a death grip on that tail, the armadillo will gain his freedom during his brief, violent struggle, and your chances of regaining your hold on that tail are zero. He will run to the nearest hole and be gone for good. For sure, he knows where all of the below-ground sanctuaries are in his domain.

So this is the proper, most tried and true way to catch an armadillo. But poor Willie employed a different, almost hopeless method. He set out right then and there to run him down. I have never seen this technique work. He bounded off the porch of his house, and the race was on. Willie, if not mentally speedy, was surprisingly fast on his feet.

The victim didn't detect the approaching predator until Willie was halfway there. When the prehistoric-looking creature finally realized he was being chased, the race was on. A cow lot is a good place for such a contest because a spectator can follow the event easily. But bare-ground, open cow lots don't go on forever. Most all such fields of play are surrounded by weeds, growing mightily in the nearby fertile soil. The armadillo was only about 5 yards ahead of Willie when he reached the waist-high careless weeds, but Willie was gaining on his prey, or seemed to be.

About ten yards into the weed patch, Willie came to a convincing, abrupt halt. He gave a sharp yelp of pain and bent over to grab his legs. I rushed to the site as Willie, badly crippled now, retraced his steps out of the weed jungle to the open area of the cow lot. He was holding, as best he could, both shins. He had slammed into a hidden plow with his lower legs. That diamond-shaped three-inch horizontal tool bar on an old plow had left half-inch deep depressions in both shins. His pain was so great Willie could barely get his breath. Taking a severe lick on your legs just below the knees is about as excruciating as anything you can experience. I felt great empathy for his plight. All I could do was stand there and pat him on the back.

But I started out talking about gaining wisdom from most anyone. Here was Willie, a borderline retarded soul, who at that moment of agony coined a term that could be applied to all the do-over stories told previously. In his great anguish, Willie's wise words were immortal. I have employed their use many times since.

He said, simply, easily, and honestly in perfectly understandable words:

"Oh. I wish I hadn't done that."

How many times could that humble statement be applied to those do-over times in my own life?

CLASSIC INSULTS

Every now and then, I stumble across something somewhere which shows a collection of classic insults attributed to famous people. Such stingers are always a hoot, and I marvel at the talent of those who created them. Winston Churchill must have been pretty darn clever because most every batch will credit the English prime minister with several gems.

Here are some of his best:

"I am enclosing two tickets to the first night of my new play; bring a friend ... if you have one."

— George Bernard Shaw, playwright (to Churchill)

"Cannot possibly attend first night; will attend second, if there is one."

— Churchill's response

An old battleax of a woman said to Winston Churchill, "If you were my husband, I would put poison in your tea." Churchill's response, "Ma'am, if you were my wife I would drink it."

— Winston Churchill

"Yes, madam, I am drunk. But in the morning I will be sober and you will still be ugly."

— Winston Churchill

Classic Insults

There are many more equally caustic attacks by intellects other than Churchill.

Now masquerading as a vagabond author, I must be alert for cutting statements such as this one:

"Thank you for sending me a copy of your book. I'll waste no time reading it."

— Moses Hadas

I marvel at minds which can create such statements out of thin air. I cannot think that fast. If a perfect retort does happen to enter my brain, it will be hours later. Such tardiness is of no use. I have always admired those who can think on their feet. You win no points when you start out by saying: "What I SHOULD HAVE SAID was - - -." Your response might be quite brilliant, but time on the game clock ran out long ago and the intended recipient has vanished. A lost opportunity is rarely made up.

Over the years, I have collected a few dandy insults which just seemed to happen perfectly at the time I heard them. They came from ordinary people living ordinary lives. In the blink of an eye, the insult was created. It was perfect. It fit like a glove. And, above all, it was true.

To make the following insults in my collection more understandable, a bit of instructive background information is provided with each classic slur to illuminate the subject. Admittedly, in some of the accounts listed below, the recipient of the insult wasn't present. But that is really not so important. Simply add that doozy to your quiver of digs to be used when an opportunity presents itself. When it comes to memorable insults, plagiarism is entirely acceptable.

The Fast Calf

Hal Churchill and I once went to a jackpot calf roping in Lampasas, over in central Texas. The roping arena was exceptionally long – half again longer than most others in use at the time. One unfortunate competitor got outrun all the way to the back gate. He never even got close enough to think about casting his loop at the fleeing calf.

Dejectedly, he was returning to the chute end of the arena and happened to pass close to the flagger of the roping. Most flaggers are, or were, calf ropers themselves and therefore have a good working knowledge of the sport. They sit astride their horse in the arena to move near the action for a close-up view of a contestant as he ties his calf.

As he passed by the flagger, the unfortunate roper, hoping for some badly-needed sympathy, said sadly, "Man, that calf sure did run, didn't he?" His entry fee had gone with the wind, and he was eager for an encouraging word.

The wily veteran of many, many calf roping contests replied with a subtle insult on the speed of the roper's horse. The flagger noted, "Yep, he sure did. And there is no telling how fast that calf would have gone if you had ever got close enough to scare him."

The Not-So-Big Buck

Since our home ranch west of San Angelo had zero deer when I was a teenager, my dad would find a deer lease somewhere to introduce me to the sport. I harvested my first-ever buck near Llano when I was 11 years old. A few years later, Dad, together with a couple of other fathers of sons about my age,

Classic Insults

found a lease on the Gerald Nix ranch west of Sonora. The best part of the deal was that Gerald's son, James, was about our age and, despite his youth, was an old hand at deer hunting. Living in that deer-rich environment, he was our resident expert. All of us boys thought James was a hero, and we hung on his every word when it came to anything having to do with hunting deer.

James tolerated us as best he could. After all, our fathers were his dad's paying customers, so he was obligated to be cordial to us tenderfeet. Had we all been teenaged girls, he would have taken more interest in us. For one thing, James could see a deer at incredible distances – much farther than I ever even looked for them. He could spot a grazing deer on the side of a hill where all I saw were trees. He would semi-patiently, finally, finally show me the distant deer. "See that big oak tree about halfway up the hill? Look 100 yards to the left now and the deer is standing by that flat-topped cedar tree." I could barely find the deer in my scope while he had seen the creature with his naked eye.

At that stage in my budding hunting career, any deer with antlers looked huge to me. Hunting alone one morning, I happened to get a fatal bullet into a small four-pointer. He was anything but a trophy, but because I had done the deed all by myself, I was happy as could be. The small size of the buck did not disqualify him as a real prize to my amateur career.

With my big, old monster in the back of the jeep, we ran onto James on the main road of the ranch as we made our way back to our tent camp up a canyon. We hailed him down to see the great harvest.

James wasn't much of a cheerleader, anyway, but he really took the wind out of my sails when he finally laid his eyes on my buck. The first comment out of his mouth was this one:

"What happened, Skipper?" he asked sarcastically. "Did you shoot him while he was nursing his mother?"

Few Words But Great Wisdom

I love descriptions which paint a complete picture with only a few simple words. This is a rare talent. Most of us beat around the bush, so to speak, before finally coming to the point we wanted to make. It's almost as if, when given the ball in a game of conversation, the player runs with it as long as possible. Or until he is tackled by an opponent who similarly wants to hog the floor.

Indeed, it is sometimes difficult to follow the theme of a narrator who goes on and on while you are waiting for him to come to his point. I have heard orators around a campfire digress in a half-dozen different directions so that I could no longer remember where their original story was headed.

To illustrate this concept, I once heard someone tell of his experience with a guy who had stopped by recently. He perfectly described the encounter when he said:

"The visitor stayed 45 minutes," as he completed his account, "and he talked for two hours."

On the other end of the spectrum, when a capsule statement comes along that wraps up several paragraphs or pages into few easy words, you are momentarily thunderstruck as you consider all that condensed wisdom. It takes a while to get your brain around what you just heard.

Here is a truly descriptive gem, easily applied to a number of people we all might know:

"OFTEN WRONG, BUT NEVER IN DOUBT."
This not-so-subtle insult is just "too-good" to remain unused in your play book.

Not Exactly Crazy, But –

Years ago, one of my calf roping buddies, a philosopher at heart, went to the concession stand at a rodeo to buy himself a soda pop. He happened to run into a barrel racer he barely knew, but because she was mightily upset and needed to sound-off on her grievance, he was unfortunately trapped into being the reluctant audience for her diatribe.

Back then, rodeo officials didn't pay all that much attention to the condition of the dirt in their arena. Before a performance, if the soil lacked moisture, they would bring in a water truck to sprinkle the area to hold down dust. Next, they would drag it smooth with a tractor and small plow or harrow of some kind. So when the rodeo got under way, the ground would be in perfect condition for a while.

But once the bucking horses, the ropers, and the steer wrestlers concluded their respective events, the ground looked like a herd of buffalos had passed through the arena. And almost always, the barrel racing event was held toward the end of the performance, just before the bull riding. So barrel racers were always complaining about the condition of the dirt in the arena.

Nowadays, of course, more attention is given to this situation. Some events drag the area with a tractor after every few runs. Others, like our big San Angelo rodeo, have men using rakes to smooth the ground around the barrels after every single run.

But years ago, barrel racers had to compete on rough ground and they were never – NEVER – happy about it. They would complain endlessly to anyone who would listen.

My friend, the philosopher, wasn't a willing listener there at the concession stand, but he was trapped. The girl, mightily upset, was right in front of him, only inches away, going on and on about the injustice of it all. The damn ground had made her horse stumble and cost her precious seconds on that run. She was just out of the money, and the scoundrels on the rodeo committee ought to have done a better job. It's a wonder she didn't cripple her horse. She'd play hell ever coming to that rodeo in the future.

When he was finally able to secure his freedom from the harangue, he beat a hasty retreat to the sanctuary of the calf roping chutes and told us of his encounter with the upset barrel racer. He wasn't convinced of her mental stability. He remembered that she had been right in his face the entire time and because she was a rather tall girl, he summed it up thusly:

"I'm here to tell you, fellows," he noted. "I was looking her right in both eyes," he went on descriptively, "and there ain't nobody home."

You Gotta Hurry

Back in my college days when I was just beginning to gain a few skills in roping calves, we practiced at Jack Aufill's arena south of Lubbock. Several calf ropers kept their horses there and most every afternoon, there was activity in the practice arena.

One afternoon, it was my good fortune to hang out there with a couple of the real celebrities of the Texas Tech rodeo world. Clyde Fort was one of the best calf ropers around. He hailed from a famous family of ropers and was mounted on one of the legendary horses in the game. H.C. Zachry, the president of the rodeo club, was a top hand in both steer wrestling and bareback bronc riding. I considered both of them to be heroes, and I was flattered by any attention they gave me. In watching my feeble attempts that afternoon, both H.C. and Clyde decided to give me a pep talk.

"Skipper," they said. "Your problem is that you don't hurry. You rope OK, but you lollygag around as if you had all day."

Their scolding continued unabated. "Calf roping IS A TIMED EVENT," they shouted. "The winner is the cowboy who ties his calf the fastest. You don't get points for style. No one cares about anything but FAST."

H.C. Zachry

I was mightily impressed that these two stars of the Texas Tech rodeo team were taking time to tutor me. They continued with this theme on and on until finally it became my turn to rope another practice calf. As I rode into the box, getting my rope ready for the pending run, I could hear both coaches continue with their instructions. "For once this afternoon, try to hurry on this one, Skipper. Hurry, hurry, hurry." They were yelling at the top of their voices.

When I nodded my head to start the process, the calf didn't really run all that hard. With only about two swings of my rope, I caught him perfectly around the neck. But that's when my troubles began.

In getting off my horse on the right side (a new technique at the time and one I was just beginning to master), I somehow hung my foot in the stirrup and fell right on my face in front of my horse. Regaining my feet as quickly as I could, with voices all around hollering at me to hurry, I darted toward the calf and got my hands on him.

But when I flanked him, I stumbled backward and the calf fell right across my legs, pinning me to the ground. As best I could, I wiggled out from under the calf and began to tie him. My hurrying caused me to fumble the procedure badly. Finally, after a couple of aborted efforts at speed, I finally had to slow down to complete the deal.

From start to finish, I had done my best to hurry, to my mind anyway. Yes, mistakes had been made all along the way, but by golly I was hurrying. Anyone could see that, I imagined.

While walking back to my horse, I looked over at the nearby coaches in hopes of an encouraging word of some kind for my attempt at "hurrying."

I asked, "Well?"

H.C. Zachry, with a look somewhere between pity and disgust, coined a term at that moment that I never forgot. He noted quite simply: "Lightning will never impress me again."

The Speeding Ticket

My buddy, Roy Green, has been in the oil business for years. He owns and operates, as best I understand it, a string of scattered oil wells. Unlike the major oil companies who have crews to do all the heavy lifting and hard, dirty work, Roy has done most of that himself for years. I doubt there is anything about an oil well he doesn't know.

One amusing thing about Roy is his choice of shirts. Because his work is incredibly hard on clothes, Roy buys old shirts from a company that supplies uniforms to various businesses. When the shirts get too old or too frayed or too shop-worn, the company disposes of them at huge discounts. Naturally, companies want their employees to look their best, and it simply wouldn't do for anyone to wear a worn-out shirt.

Except for Roy. He is their No. 1 customer for the old shirts. They are perfect for the grimy work he has facing him around the oil wells. The problem is that most of the worn-out shirts have some employee's name embroidered over the front pocket. So when I run into Roy somewhere, he might be "John" one day and "Sam" the next. Beyond these names, Roy has a variety of CB radio handles. I have heard him called "Red-Neck Roy" or "Digger Green." Back in the days when he and his wife, Margaret, would go snow skiing, Roy called himself "Spider." So Roy Green has a multitude of names.

He has an equal number of communication devices in his truck. There's

Roy Green

his CB radio, of course, plus there is a two-way radio with a large speaker. Since he hates and simply cannot stand to get a speeding ticket, he employs the use of one or two radar detectors, as well. And nowadays, of course, Roy has his laptop computer and a cell phone. The top of his old Dodge truck is peppered with antennae of various types and sizes.

Out north of San Angelo, the devious highway patrolmen are constantly lurking near an area where, all of a sudden, the 70 mph speed limit is reduced to 60 mph for a mile or two. Roy is on that road often – no, more than often – he is on that road constantly as he comes and goes from his "digs," as he calls his string of oil wells. Those things need Roy's constant, regular attention for this one simple reason: If they ain't-a pumping no oil, he ain't-a making no money. So he's running here and there to get this or that part to keep the oil flowing into his tanks. And therefore, he's on that road where the cops roam on a regular basis.

And, as you would probably suspect, when Roy needs a part of some kind, he is in a hurry to get the thing in order to get that well back on line.

On one memorable occasion, Roy was flying down the highway when, all of a sudden and from out of nowhere, a black and white pulls him over. Just his luck.

The cop walks up to Roy's old truck with all those antennae sticking out everywhere. As he approaches the window where the dejected Roy is waiting to get his well-deserved speeding ticket, the cop creates a classic insult for poor old Roy. The patrolman twists the dagger a bit when he observes:

"Man. With all those antennae you have on this truck, it looks like you would have known I was in the area."

Two-Way Radios

It's difficult to remember now, but there was a time, not so long ago really, when cell phones didn't exist. But we humans crave communication. Ever since the days of the Indians and their smoke signals, new technology is eagerly accepted when it comes along.

So it was when two-way radios were in frequent use. For those whose work was done miles and miles out in the West Texas wilderness, these devices were a Godsend. Most oil field trucks were equipped with them, but a fair number of ranchers had the things, too. They were much larger and more powerful than the CB radios used by truckers. But it was the same "push-to-talk" type deal. You depressed a button on a microphone to enable you to send your message for scores of miles in most locations.

There was another interesting feature about these devices. They had "channels" on which the communication flowed. Some of the more expensive and sophisticated setups would limit the conversation only to their desired frequency bands. But on most two-way radios, you heard whoever was talking to whomever, and the babble would almost be constant.

Andy Smith had one of the devices in his truck. It was great entertainment to listen to all the conversations going on, similar to the days of yore when there were "party-line telephones." The radio in the cab of his truck kept up an endless chatter. You finally learned to "tune out" unnecessary dialogues, but for entertainment purposes, you just might hear a hoot of a conversation.

Andy remembered that Friday afternoons were particularly interesting as the oil field troops were returning to town and using their radios to line up dates that night with female companions. He tried to listen in whenever he could. You would think that the conversationalists would realize that their talk was being heard by everyone on the system, but that rarely bothered anyone. Somehow they just assumed that the talk was private.

On one memorable such afternoon, Andy was monitoring his radio just to see what might unfold. Here is what Andy heard as one Romeo successfully reached his girlfriend on her radio:

Romeo: " Hey, sugar. What's up?"

Female voice: "Not much."

Romeo: "Oh yeah? Not much, eh?"

Female voice: "No, not much. My ex-husband was just over here for a while."

Romeo, now somewhat alarmed: "Your ex-husband?"

Female voice: "Yeah, my ex was here."

Romeo, now instantly suspicious: "Why, that rascal. What did he want?"

Female voice, coyly: "You know what he wanted."

Andy turned up the volume on his radio so as not to miss a word of this dialog. There was a longer-than-usual pause in the discourse.

Romeo, now obviously alarmed: "Now wait just a minute." Andy could hear the panic in his voice. "You didn't give it to him, did you?"

Female voice, now a bit condescending: "I never turned you down, did I?"

Andy almost lost control of his pickup after that one.

Classic insults can sometimes be a bit subtle, but the next two won't be.

The Harley-Davidson Man

Jim Schwarz worked around our hunting camp as both a guide and a cook for a number of years. Being a Green Beret on three tours in Vietnam and having been a long-haul trucker, a cowboy, and a bass fishing guide to boot, Jim was full of stories as you might imagine.

Because he had lived among the Montagnard tribesmen in Viet Nam for years, I once asked him during lunch on day to describe the strangest meal he ate with them. Setting his fork down momentarily as he considered the question, he finally guessed that a monkey might be the most unusual thing he had eaten with his hosts. "Wow," I said in amazement. "A monkey? What does a monkey taste like?"

Jim had a ready answer: "Kind of like a house cat."

By now, Jim had become a true Harley-Davidson man. Not only did he own the largest, blackest bike made by that company, their famous logo could be found plastered all over his truck and any place else he could find to stick one. Just to get my ire up, he wore an earring as he arrived on his Harley for our annual landowner supper. Thank goodness it was a magnet-type and hadn't required a hole in his ear. He grumbled as I "suggested" he remove the offensive trinket.

One spring, Jim was cooking for us. A big shindig had been planned for numerous important guests. We hoped they would be promoting our spring turkey hunting. For the occasion, I was not surprised to see that Jim's choice of dress was a black T-shirt with a huge Harley logo.

Larry Meeks, one of our guides who had unfortunately lost his wife to cancer sometime back, had begun to date the widow of his college teammate. The two friends had played football at UTEP in El Paso. The widow, Linda, was meeting all our Adobe Lodge crew for the first time. Finally, she was introduced to Jim Schwarz.

She couldn't help but notice his shirt, and she asked politely, "Nice to meet you, Jim. Do you ride motorcycles?"

Jim's chest swelled a few inches. "Sure do," he claimed proudly. Finally, someone had noticed.

Linda easily carried the conversation forward as she noted reflectively, "My late husband and I rode motorcycles for years."

Just like a bird dog getting a tell-tale scent, Jim immediately picked up on this bulletin. "So you used to ride motorcycles?" he asked hopefully.

"Yep, we rode them everywhere." Linda was quickly making a huge impression on Jim Schwarz.

Jim had found a true compatriot. He was overjoyed at finding a blood-sister, so to speak. He pressed on for details and was eager to know more.

"What kind of motorcycle did you ride, Linda?" That would easily be the first question one biker would want to know about another.

Perfectly at ease among all the strangers in her midst, Linda replied factually to the query. "I rode a Kawasaki."

The color drained out of Jim's ruddy face at this bombshell. He almost lost his breath on that one, but recovered enough to continue with his line of questioning.

"A Kawasaki?" He couldn't believe what he was hearing. "Why in the world would you ride a Kawasaki?"

For all of us within the range of hearing on that momentous day, Linda's answer was flawless as she adroitly deflated that mystique perpetrated by Jim Schwarz. He would never be the same.

Without even pausing to think about it, she replied perfectly: "Well, someone had to have a way to go get parts for all those old Harleys."

★ ★ ★

Classic Insults

The Personal Trainer

Roy Don Scott is easily the best musician I was ever privileged to pick along with over the years. From old country-western ballads to Broadway show tunes and everything in between, Roy Don has mastered them all. And he remembers the words to hundreds of tunes.

When Roy Don was approaching retirement age, he divested himself of his business interests. Not only could he spend more time with his music, he plunged whole-heartedly into physical fitness. He joined a health club and turned out to be one of their most frequent participants. In addition to their programs of aerobic conditioning, Roy Don also spent considerable time in their weight room. After a few years of this regimen, he could hoist impressive amounts of dead weight. On the rare days not spent at the gym, he might be found walking for miles and miles.

To underscore his seriousness about his program, he even solicited the help of a personal trainer. As it so happened, he was assigned an attractive female who was delighted to help someone as motivated as Roy Don.

One memorable day, the pretty trainer, decades younger than R.D., was helping him with a particular set of weights. As it so happened, an exceptionally muscled-up male client of that establishment cruised by their activity

Roy Don Scott

area. That young girl trainer sighed at the sight of the Atlas-like creature as he wandered off. She said, mostly to herself, "Wow. What a hunk he is."

Roy Don, ever the prankster, had to counter this obvious display of female infatuation. An idea came to his fertile mind.

"Now wait just a minute there," challenged R.D. "I take exception to that."

"What do you mean?" wondered the star-stricken trainer.

Roy Don went on with his thought. "Well, now. When it comes to just pure, passionate, unadulterated SEX," he asked provocatively, "what's HE GOT, that I don't have?"

The girl trainer put Roy Don down for the count with her answer. "Probably a partner."

Dynamite Stories

When stories begin to flow around a campfire, sooner or later a tale or two about dynamite will be told. I have heard or read several versions of the following yarn:

A duck hunter arrived at a frozen pond. With no open water available, he quickly realized that ducks would bypass this particular lake. So, with a bountiful duck harvest as his goal, as the story goes, he just happened to have a stick of dynamite. He lit the thing and cast it as far as he could out on the frozen surface in an attempt "to make water" to attract his feathered prey.

Sounds like a workable plan, doesn't it?

Unfortunately, his well-trained retriever dog bounded out on the ice to eagerly fetch the missile back to his horrified owner. Sensing immediate danger, the hunter shouted commands and threats at the top of his voice, all to no avail. The poor, confused dog, carrying the explosive package in his mouth, headed for the nearest sanctuary where he would be safe from the tirade – underneath his owner's brand new Suburban.

Whether or not this story has validity, I have no clue.

Since I have no personal experience with anything larger than firecrackers, I am always a keen listener when dynamite is discussed. I was scared to death of the stuff well before I heard the following historical lectures from credible friends:

★ ★ ★

Tommy Nasworthy

I first got to know Tommy Nasworthy while I was in high school. My dad had secured a deer lease on his Menard ranch, about 75 miles southeast of San Angelo. As my interest in ranching, cowboying and calf roping grew, Tommy, who was ten years older, became my mentor and consultant for all these activities. I visited him and his family as often as I could. Each trip was educational to say the least, and I always learned a-plenty from my time with him.

Back before about the mid-1950s, all the land between San Angelo and the lake belonged to the Nasworthy family. In fact, several of the Nasworthy pastures ran right to the city limits. San Angelo's College Hills, Southland and Bentwood additions were all once part of the original Nasworthy ranch. As best I remember, their old headquarters would have been somewhere in the middle of

Tommy Nasworthy

the Southland neighborhood. That land was sold off piece by piece over the years as the growth of the city took dead-aim on their ranch land. Being ranchers at heart, Tommy and his father, Dick, used those proceeds to acquire their Menard property.

Having just graduated from high school, Tommy was living on that old home place ranch south of the city. He was the primary ranch hand for his dad and his uncles. In cleaning out an old barn one day, he came across a most unusual and dangerous box. It was packed with sticks of dynamite. Where and how that stuff came to be there was of little concern to Tommy. His most immediate question was: How in the world do you get rid of dynamite? Surely to goodness, he didn't want that box to stay there in his barn. He couldn't just throw it into the trash pit there on the ranch. He could perhaps bury the stuff, but no rancher likes to dig holes in the ground, and it would take a big one to provide safety from that threatening box.

So he hatched a simple plan. He would carefully, gingerly haul that container out into a pasture and set it on the ground. Then, he would retreat a couple of hundred yards and shoot the box with his deer rifle. Blowing up the dangerous cargo seemed to be the wisest move. Who would ever know?

Having years of experience with guns of all kinds, it didn't take Tommy but two shots to hit the distant target. But he wasn't prepared for the resulting explosion. The boom almost shook the leaves off the mesquite trees, and there was a mighty hole left in the ground that could have swallowed his pickup. Dust and smoke billowed up and blotted out the sun, but the strong wind that day dispersed the evidence before gaining much altitude. His dynamite-disposal efforts would remain his little secret. The problem was solved, or so he thought.

Imagine his horror the next day when the local newspaper was plastered with a huge headline running the entire width of the page:

Mystery Explosion Rocks South San Angelo
Windows Broken in Several Homes

For days thereafter, law enforcement personnel followed lead after lead in their quest to solve the riddle. Characteristically, Tommy never 'fessed up.

The Cesspool

In southeastern New Mexico, the dirt is pretty sandy. During the oil boom of the 1950s, housing was in short supply and there was a rush to meet the demand. With all that sandy and porous soil on the small-acreage places outside of town, many of the builders did not go to the trouble of installing proper septic tanks with drain lines. They simply dug a big pit – called a cesspool – for the waste produced by the household. The void would be covered securely to reduce any offensive odors. The ensuing sewage disposal worked fine until, after time, the sides and the bottom of the pit became impervious to water. Sooner or later, the pit would get full and you needed to pump it out – an expensive, disgusting, and unpleasant undertaking.

One such unfortunate victim of a full cesspool, Gus, sought advice from William Chandler who worked at a local supply house which handled products of various kinds. Gus wanted to rent a pump to empty his cesspool. William was eager to help but admitted that they had no pumps for rent. Furthermore, he knew of no chemicals that would have the desired effect. He did, however, have an idea for Gus to try. He had heard of a simple, yet effective method to cure that particular problem.

"There is really nothing to it," William assured Gus. "Here's what you do. Get yourself a couple of sticks of dynamite and duct-tape them together. Next, find a softball-size rock and tie those sticks to the rock. You'll want to use a fuse with a decent length. The fuse will continue to burn even when wet."

Gus was all ears as William continue his instructions. "Light the fuse and lob the bomb into the exact middle of the surface. When the rock carries the dynamite to the bottom of your cesspool, with all that sludge above to absorb the blast, the explosion will crack all the sides of the hole and the bottom, too. The water will drain quickly, and your problem will be solved."

"What a hell of an idea," thought Gus. "What could be easier? Or cheaper?" He secured a couple of sticks of dynamite and a fuse that, he was told, would burn for at least 30 seconds – plenty of time for the bomb to sink to the bottom of the pit.

He had, with considerable trouble, already removed the cover over his cesspool. Underneath several inches of sand, he had found several long poles covered with tin from an old barn. The resultant barrier wasn't pretty but had been effective when it came to odors, especially since the pit was situated only a few yards away from his stucco dwelling. The pit was obviously completely full, and indeed, plumbing in his house was backing up and hardly draining at all. This was a crisis that called for an immediate solution. Thanks to William, he now had the answer.

So armed with the dynamite, the fuse and the rock, he could effectively solve his problem. He constructed the missile carefully according to William's instruction. He lit the fuse and heaved the package out into the center of the pit. But immediately, a huge problem arose.

During the short flight of the bomb, the rock disengaged itself from the dynamite sticks and promptly disappeared from sight out there in the middle of the hole. The explosive package of dynamite sticks floated easily on top of the muck, the fuse burning away rapidly. Sensing an impending massive explosion, Gus ran as fast as his legs would carry him.

The detonation, when it came, was a big one. Brown crud flew in all directions. Tragically, the nearby white house had a brand new color.

The only good news was that the cesspool was no longer completely full.

Rattlesnakes and Dynamite

Back in the 1960s when Andy Smith was fully occupied with his family's extensive sheep business, he found several rattlesnake dens on their ranch, about 30 miles west of San Angelo. During the busy lamb-marking season in February, his horseback tours had taken him by several rocky bluffs. The actual dens of the snakes are fairly easy to spot. Most all of them face the south, and the ground outside the den will be rubbed smooth as the snakes exit their cave to enjoy an occasional warm spring day. By late March or so, the snakes abandon their winter quarters as the days grow longer and warmer.

Once the lamb-marking was done, Andy invited some friends to assist with a "rattlesnake extermination" in his efforts to reduce the serpents' numbers on the ranch. Roy Green, Stormy Kimrey and Corky Shelby were willing participants in the adventure. Andy simply wanted to eliminate the critters. The others thought they might catch a few of the reptiles to see if a market for live snakes might be found.

Not all the holes and caverns in a bluff are snake dens. Some are; some aren't. It's best to verify the presence of snakes by actually seeing them. Snake hunters use a small mirror to catch sunlight and direct it into a hole. The resultant beam is brighter than a spotlight and the snakes are easily seen if they are there.

Andy had heard of a new method of encouraging the snakes to leave their den, even on a day that is not sunny and warm. The idea was to pump gasoline into the very back of the den. Snakes don't like gasoline and will do their best to get away from the fumes. So the trick is this: Attach a long copper tube to a garden sprayer filled with gasoline. Run the tube into a den as far back as you can possibly get it to go. Then pump the fluid behind the snakes. They exit the hole at the entrance to the den where they can either be captured or killed easily.

So Andy and his three accomplices soon found a nice den. The mirrors confirmed that, indeed, the hole contained a goodly number of snakes. The tube was inserted; the gasoline was pumped. But after a reasonable amount of time, no snakes had exited the den. In analyzing the situation, the team of four concluded that the tube had failed to reach the back of the den. The gasoline had most probably been squirted between the snakes and the opening, thereby driving the serpents even further into the hole.

They had botched the deal.

But Andy cared nothing about capturing the snakes. Extermination was on his mind. Stormy Kimrey came prepared for just such a problem. He had brought along a generous supply of dynamite. Just the ticket, thought Andy. A stick would be placed in that hole and the entire snake den would be blown to smithereens. The rattlesnake extermination program would be under way.

So that's what they did. Stormy, who knew a little something about dynamite, showed Andy how to prepare the charge. Use a sharp tool to poke a hole into the end of the stick of dynamite. Insert a dynamite cap and a length of fuse. Crimp everything tightly, and you're ready to go. They succeeded in pushing the package well into the hole. Now it was time to light the end of the fuse right there at the opening of the hole.

When poor Andy struck a match to start the fuse, he had forgotten that the den was still full of vapors from the gasoline. Immediately, the flame of the match causes the fumes to explode with a horrendous "whomph." The dynamite, thankfully, did not go off, but the near-disaster of the gasoline's ignition so un-nerved Andy that he immediately withdrew from the game.

Roy Green, Stormy Kimrey and Corky Shelby soldiered on with the task of ridding Andy's ranch of rattlesnakes.

It wasn't long before another den was found. The gasoline injection method was tried once again with similarly unproductive results. No snakes exited the den. Now what? The new committee of three held a brief meeting. The unanimous decision was easy – it was time to implode the den and send all the snakes to their doom. The non-voting fourth member, Andy, was watching from a safe distance in the sanctuary of his pickup cab, keeping tabs on all the children who were along for the adventure.

But now, everyone remembered Andy's misfortune with the match and the gasoline. Using an old gunny sack as a torch, it was dropped into a crevice over the den. The gasoline fumes were successfully ignited and disposed of. It was time to insert the dynamite. Because the cliff area was rather large, the consulting expert of the group, Stormy, determined that six sticks of dynamite would be required to destroy the den.

The explosive package was affixed to long limb to be pushed well back into the hole where the snakes lurked. A decent length of fuse was used, to be sure. But somehow, and the details still remain unclear, the fuse burned extra-fast once it was ignited. Immediately, it became important to get the hell away as fast as possible. It seemed as if the cavern acted similar to the barrel of a mortar. Being situated up the hill, Stormy simply stepped to one side and was fairly safe. Being located downhill, Roy tried to outrun the explosion but didn't quite gain as much distance as he wanted. When the eruption came, rocks the size of basketballs were falling all around as he ran for his life. In horror, Andy watched the entire fiasco from the safety of his truck. No, Roy didn't get whacked by any boulders, but his heart rate quadrupled.

The moral of this tale is simple:

Despite their best efforts that day, rattlesnakes on Andy's ranch were not going to be added to the endangered species list.

It was the four snake exterminators with their dynamite who gained that honor.

Running Stories

Allen Hamblen – Runner

Max Sanders is the guilty party who started me on my running career.

When I quit roping calves, I felt the need to find a way to stay in shape. I hadn't realized how much physical demands the sport of roping had put on me. On the rare occasions when I would "come out of retirement" and tie down a few head, I was sore in places I didn't even know I had. So maintaining some kind of physical conditioning seemed to be important. Max, who had practiced recreational running for years and even possesses a doctorate in exercise physiology, goaded me into at least trying to run.

Trouble was, I had been a lifelong asthmatic. Any quick exertion would bring on an attack. Before a roping event, I would habitually take a couple of hits from my ever-present "whiffer" – the albuterol inhaler I always carried in my back pocket. So I protested to Max that my asthma would prohibit any kind of sustained running.

Max, of course, pooh-poohed such excuses. And being a master at laying on guilt trips, he finally succeeded in getting me out the door and onto the road.

One day, I ran away from the house and, using the whiffer to halt any asthma, made almost a quarter of a mile before I was totally winded. Over the next several weeks, I gradually increased the distance to a mile, then two miles, and within a few months, I could actually run to the main gate of the ranch and back – a total of five miles.

What a feeling of accomplishment that was. Best of all, my asthma had virtually disappeared. I was amazed and heartened by this development. After that first year of steady workouts, I was hooked on running.

Come to find out, some of my friends were getting into the activity as well. No longer hanging out with blue jean- and spur-wearing cowboys with their big hats, my new compatriots wore shorts and running shoes. Conversations dwelt on miles-per-week and training runs. Every so often, a local race was held and we would all enter to see just what our "official time" might be over a carefully measured distance.

One of my friends who took up running at that time was Dr. Bob Hamblen, the anesthesiologist. In addition to our running activities, we were regular companions on numerous quail hunts during bird season. Other times of the year, running dominated our conversations.

Those addicted to the sport dwell endlessly on their training regimen. They talk incessantly of the miles they run. This minutia crops up in almost every conversation. Whenever Bob and I were together, we would compare notes on this topic while waiting for quail season to finally arrive.

Bob's younger son, Allen, was about 8 years old at the time. Allen, an extrovert like his dad, would listen to our conversations with rapt attention. But being an unrepentant and tireless talker, he would try his best to weigh in on all the exchanges, almost always to no avail. Good as he was or tried to be, he couldn't compete with his dad. Allen could hardly get a word in edgewise. Who wants to listen to a kid anyway when there are weighty matters of miles-run to discuss?

On one memorable occasion when I visited Bob at his house in town, little Allen was determined to get in his two-bit's worth. When a break finally came in the conversation between Bob and me, Allen seized the moment as his own. He announced proudly that just that very morning, he had succeeded in "running 40 yards." Once this solemn declaration had been made, he waited expectantly for some affirmation of his momentous feat by his elders. When none came, he repeated the claim.

"This morning" he said ever more loudly and distinctly, "I ran 40 yards."

Now, finally, he had our attention. Wanting to offer some kind of encouraging comment to the youngster, both Bob and I offered meager praise for his accomplishment but without any real admiration. Good grief. Forty yards? What is so special about that?

Allen sensed our lack of enthusiasm. He could tell that neither of us was properly impressed. But he continued to be proud of his feat. Somehow, he needed to get it all into an impressive, appropriate perspective. He found an effective way to do just that by recounting his triumph for the third time. This time it worked. Both Bob and I finally grasped the scope of his deed when he said:

"And that doesn't even count the driveways I crossed when I ran through those 40 yards." The yards in Bob's neighborhood were pretty doggoned big, too – not the miniscule yards you might find in front of town houses. Those 40 yards might have totaled way over a mile. Maybe two.

Charlie Bob Stryker, Non-Runner

For years and years, one of the best bluegrass music festivals in Texas was to be found at Glen Rose, about 60 miles southwest of Fort Worth. Held over the Memorial Day weekend, the weather was usually pretty good. Oh yeah, it would be hot during the day, but the nights were just perfect as jam sessions got under way throughout the large campground. A music lover could wander from group to group and get a front-row experience as good as what might be heard on the stage by the professional bands in attendance.

In that venue, it wasn't long until I came to know Eddie Pitman. Eddie lived up north of the Dallas-Fort Worth Metroplex and was a small-town banker. But, for some reason, he never used his own name. He had concocted a better name for use among his musician buddies – Charlie Bob Stryker. Maybe he thought that moniker would be a better fit around bluegrass music.

Where the name originated was never made clear to me, but he introduced himself to one and all with that handle, in that exact manner. In meeting a new face one time, and during the introduction, the newcomer said, "It's nice to meet you, Charlie."

He was swiftly corrected by the bearer of the name. "That's Charlie BOB." Embarrassed with his faux pas, the stranger quickly corrected himself and apologized profusely. "Sorry, CHARLIE BOB. I'll get it right from now on." And he did. And so did the rest of us.

Charlie Bob was a big guy, a bit overweight bordering on pudgy. His appearance was magnified by his choice of dress – bib overalls. He looked more like a mule trader than a banker. But he was a stellar member of our group of rank amateur, barely-competent musicians. We spent lots of time in jam-session circles during the three-day event. No, frankly, we weren't worth a damn, but no one enjoyed playing more than our little bunch. It was great practice to hone our limited skills. Charlie Bob played a guitar and knew the words to a million songs – a valuable asset at a music festival. But unlike the rest of us who camped out in tents or rattletrap trailers, Charlie Bob owned a huge, Class A motor home which was more appropriate for his alter-ego, Eddie Pitman, the banker.

But never mind his opulent housing. He was a country boy at heart. During lulls in the music, he could talk for hours about his experiences years ago with his pack of coonhounds – a pastime more suited to someone named "Charlie Bob" than a banker. Most all hound dog men are extremely easy going and patient people. They are rarely in a rush about anything. Charlie Bob fit this description to a tee.

In addition to being addicted to bluegrass music in those days, my other pastime was running. Similar to my music, I was way back in the pack with skills in either hobby. I could neither play music well nor run very fast, but no matter. I did the best I could and spent all my spare time at one or the other diversion.

So at the Glen Rose festival one morning just at daybreak, I went out for a quick five-mile run before the main music events of the day got under way. Yes, the air was cooler at that early hour, but the humidity was plenty high. So I worked up a mighty sweat in the process. As I ended the run at the gate to the park where everyone was camped, and as I made my way to my camping spot, I was dripping as if I had been swimming in the nearby Paluxy River. Walking slowly to try to drip-dry as much as possible, I just happened to pass by Charlie Bob's camper bus. He was sitting in a lawn chair on the shady side of the huge rig enjoying a cup of coffee while his wife was making breakfast inside. I could smell bacon cooking.

Because we were only casual acquaintances at those music festivals, Charlie Bob had no idea that I was a runner. He was aghast at my appearance walking along there by his rig wearing nothing but my running shorts and shoes, still as wet as if I had been sprayed by a water hose.

"Good grief, Skipper," he exclaimed. "What in the hell happened to you? You are as wet as a catfish."

By now I had caught my breath and words came easily. "I've been running, Charlie Bob."

He couldn't believe his ears. "Running! Running! What the hell for? Was somebody after you?"

Amused at his response, I set him straight. "No, no. I just went out jogging. I ran about five miles since daylight."

"Running? Jogging? " Charlie Bob couldn't believe his ears or the evidence he was seeing. "What the hell are you running for?"

"Well," I continued, "running is supposed to be good for you, Charlie Bob. Makes you healthy and all that."

Charlie Bob took a sip of his coffee to give him time to consider this bulletin. It was easy to see that he had totally rejected the report.

He said emphatically, "No, no, Skipper. Running is NOT good for you. I know that for a fact. You need to quit all that foolishness."

"Oh, yeah?" I was getting defensive. "Just how do you know that running isn't good for you?"

"That's easy," Charlie Bob counseled patiently. "I tried it one time AND I GOT PLUMB OUT OF BREATH."

Knowing Charlie Bob, he needed to save every breath he had for the songs he would be singing the rest of the day and night.

Horse Trading

A Brief Look at the Rules

When a buyer is dickering with a seller on something, the process seems to be universally known as "Horse Trading," no matter the nature of the product. Many people love to play this game, and it is practiced around the world whether you are in an outdoor market in Ethiopia or in a mule barn in Missouri.

I'm not much of a trader. Never was any good at it, for a variety of reasons. For one thing, if I am buying a horse, a cow, a dog or a truck, my plan is to keep it forever. I don't have plans to re-sell the thing in the near future.

Not so with traders. When they make a purchase, almost immediately that item is put up for sale at a price that will turn a profit. I once heard of a cattleman whose idea of a long-term plan was limited to what he might do with the bovines over the weekend.

Not being a trader myself, I still have a few observations about the species since I have been around a-plenty of them. Because their approach is always so much different than mine, I am continually fascinated with that breed and how they play their complicated game. I just barely understand the rules. Over the years, I've observed that there seem to be some guidelines to follow, whether you are bargaining for horses, cattle, trucks, guns, or whatever. Just to keep things constant, the following examples will assume it's horse trading.

First of all, a price must be established. It is totally out of bounds to ask a potential buyer: "What will you give me for him?" A "Foundation Rule" has been broken. The old pro's response invariably will be: "I don't make it a habit to price another man's horse. You tell me what you want for him." And, then, as night follows day, when the seller finally offers up a price that he imagines is "fair," the buyer will feign horror at such an exorbitant figure, even if he secretly considers the price to be a bargain. The buyer will do his best to try to get a much lower price. It's all a part of the game he loves to play, and he will employ a variety of gambits to win the contest.

During the buying process, for example, real traders are masters at criticizing the seller's product. For this segment, let's assume an experienced horse buyer is matched against a novice horse seller. The buyer will find so many faults with the nag under consideration that one wonders why he would even want the poor, blemished thing in the first place. He will point out every flaw he sees, either real or imagined. The purpose of this harsh critique, of course, is to intimidate the seller thereby destroying his pride in his animal. His insinuation is this: The horse is barely worth buying. Realistically, the horse is worth next-to-nothing. This is another reason I would never make a horse trader. When my horse is criticized by a potential buyer, I take it to heart. Yes, I know harsh appraisals are all a part of the charade, but I never liked it.

If the seller is a greenhorn, this harangue is almost always effective. He will begin to question his own asking price. Maybe it is too high, after all. Like the ever-present

GPS units, he immediately begins "recalculating." Already, the clever buyer is way ahead on points.

The next step in the process is the offer by the buyer. It has already been established by now that the asking price is out of the question. The potential buyer is now obligated to bid on the animal, and, no surprise here, his offer will be way, way below what the seller hoped to get. Among their own kind, horse traders candidly refer to this segment as "I shot him in the knee." Now the unfortunate seller is in a real dilemma. His horse, according to this supposedly knowledgeable buyer, is worth nowhere near what he had assumed. As he remembers all the faults and blemishes found by the buyer, he might be discouraged enough to accept the offer and go home to lick his wounds.

Or, if he is brave enough, he might lower his asking price hoping for a more reasonable offer. When the new, lower price is suggested, the buyer will wail and moan and assure the seller that he has already made his best offer, but he truly, truly wants to help. So he ups his offer by a miniscule amount, all the while promising the seller that there is no way the horse is worth the offer, but he is being overly generous and will regret his charity tomorrow.

The poor novice is out of his league and has no chance in the matchup. He will lose as surely as the NFL champions would hammer your high school football team.

Now, let's turn the situation around 180 degrees. The beginner is interested in a horse owned by the wily trader, the seller in this example. The clever vendor will brag and brag on every positive attribute of the animal, both actual and imaginary. His library of catchy sales pitches runneth over. Good grief. He could recount his speech in his sleep. Seldom, he confides to the buyer, has he ever offered a horse of this quality for sale. Truthfully, he goes on, he is sorely tempted to keep the pony for his own personal use. And, of course, he has priced the horse way, way above his bottom dollar. If the novice is on a budget and mentions that he can only pay so much, and if that proposed offer still yields a tidy profit to the trader, it will be accepted only after the trader has made another couple of attempts to squeeze even more money out of the buyer.

Time is on the side of the horse trader. Since there is no play clock in this complicated game, he will dicker with a rookie forever if he has to. But if two old pros are involved on both sides of the trade, they will still include all of the elements listed above for pure professional courtesy. Both will abbreviate the criticizing and bragging aspects with neither party taking offense at derogatory comments. Heck fire. They expected such and would be disappointed if it didn't come. Water off a duck's back. Omitting the obligatory condemnation/praise segment is akin to neglecting the Star-Spangled Banner at the Super Bowl.

Once the culmination of the trade draws close, if a buyer says, "I'll give you X amount," that becomes a binding, contractual offer and ethically, he cannot rescind the proposition. To keep himself from getting burned in this trap, an experienced buyer will come at the deal in a careful manner. He might say something like this: "Would you take X amount?" Safer yet is this question: "What's the least you would take?"

Before the buyer and seller finally reach an agreement on price, both need to be 100 percent sure they understand the deal. If you are talking cattle, there is the shrink issue to be hammered out. And what about delivery? Exactly when and where does the change in ownership take place?

I once sold a roping horse to a man from Hawaii who had come to see our big roping fiesta here in San Angelo one fall. I priced the horse, and he didn't quibble even a little. He also bought my long-shot horse trailer and again paid my asking price. But then he wondered if I would be agreeable to delivering the horse and trailer to Clovis. Since he had paid full price for both without complaint, I readily agreed. Come to find out a few hours later, he was referring to Clovis, California, not Clovis, New Mexico. Since "a deal is a deal," a concept accepted without question by all traders, I was obliged to make that long trip to the west coast. Driving that rig through the Los Angeles freeway system was a burden I would not wish on anyone. Lesson: Be sure you completely understand all aspects of the deal you make.

Actual horse trades are infinitely more complicated than the few illustrations above. It would take a book of considerable size to properly detail all the finer points of swapping and trading. Horse traders, no matter their specific product, are almost always extroverts. They are most enjoyable companions and continually full of stories. I remember some classics I have heard over the years...

Coon Hound Characters

My good buddy, Joe Henderson, back during his high school days, spent every available night hunting raccoons somewhere around San Angelo. He was addicted to the sport and introduced many of his amigos to his all-night adventures, as well.

I accompanied him on one occasion, but that was enough for me. Too much walking. Not enough sleep. Too cold. Gloom of night. Too many thorn bushes. And I never developed an ear for the baying of the hounds. Coon dog aficionados can easily discern the individual voice of a specific dog even among a half-dozen others yapping in the distance. It is music to their ears. Old joke: I could never hear the music for all the barking of the dogs. That described me to a "T." Does that stand for "tone deaf?"

My father had granted Joe Henderson unlimited coon hunting privileges on our ranch, not all that far from town. With the Middle Concho River as the northern boundary, the river bottom was a likely place to jump-up a coon. There is no telling how many nights Joe spent following a pack of dogs on our river. Years later during a fishing weekend adventure on our place, Joe revealed he was continually lost on the Middle Concho during the daylight. Had it been nighttime, he knew that stream like the back of his hand.

Joe introduced companion after companion to coon hunting. One of his favorite sources of information was "Mountain Music Magazine." Their subtitle said it all: "Published in the interest of the boys at the forks of the creek as well as the men of many mansions." In one memorable issue, Joe learned of a wild coon hunt contest to be held in East Texas. This was an irresistible lure. Joe and a few of his night-hunting companions decided to attend. One of these recruits was William Wells, who owned no dog himself but always wanted to. So it came to pass that Joe, William and a couple more coon dog lovers,

Rowdy, Joe Henderson, and Concho

Al Waggoner and Jimmy Wheeler, made the trip to enter Joe's dogs in the match.

It is simply a given. Any human who gets interested in any dog sport (coon dogs, bird dogs, sheep dogs, you name it), sooner or later must simply, positively own a dog of his very own. William Wells dreamed of owning a coon hound. As luck would have it, right there at the park where the scores of hunters set up their camps, a few "dog traders" appeared in hopes of doing a little business peddling their hounds.

The collection of mutts would be tied to a picket line stretched between tall trees. During the daylight hours before the competition got under way after dark, attendees would prowl the park to check out each other's dogs. Among the hundreds of dogs on the grounds, William just happened to fall in love with a particular hound owned by one of the traders. One has to wonder about the origin of this spark of infatuation. But it was there, no doubt. The trader, with that gift they all possess, was able to look right into the heart and soul of the hapless William. He knew for sure he had a victim – er, ah – a buyer.

His sales pitch regarding the dog was masterful. He priced the dog at $35, a respectful sum back in the 1950's, somehow knowing that was all the money William had in his wallet. (How do traders do this?) William's feeble attempts at dickering for a lower price, as anyone could have predicted, came to naught. But his obsession with this particular hound overcame his economic good sense, so he bought the dog as all his San Angelo companions watched from a distance. After enjoying the seller's generous praise for his learned judgment in acquiring one hell of a good dog, William was gratified to hear Joe and the others offer their own sincere congratulations. William finally owned a coon hound of his very own.

During the walk back to the San Angelo camp, every noticeable positive trait of the dog was reviewed over and over. Now William was an equal among peers. He could truly be known as a coon dog man. He never felt happier.

After some period of time, with William's head way in the clouds, one of the San Angelo hunters asked a profoundly important question. "William," he wondered. "What is that dog's name?"

Horror of horrors. That is the one question William had failed to ask of the dog trader. Believing in the old adage about there being bad luck in changing the name of an animal, William almost trotted back to the far side of the campground to ask the old trader this very question. Of course, the wily salesman immediately recognized his recent customer and greeted him warmly.

"Say," implored the anxious William. "I failed to ask you the name of the dog I bought." Of course, in his heart of hearts, he was hoping to learn the dog carried some clever, charismatic handle.

The crafty trader patted the wad of William's cash in his pocket, knowing that the culmination of the deal happened a full hour ago, and now he could be quite candid with the dog buyer. There was no way William could back out of the trade at this point.

"Well," he said in all honesty, "You can call him anything you want to. But I've been calling him ' OLD RABBIT.'"

Joe Henderson remembers that when the gang of coon hunters finally returned to their home hunting grounds around San Angelo, to William's everlasting disappointment, the dog was aptly named.

Tales Galore: And a Whole Lot More

The Minneapolis-Moline Tractor

Speaking of Joe Henderson, after his graduation from Texas Tech, Joe returned home to work in the family business, Porter Henderson Implement Company, a John Deere dealership established by his father. To the north, east and south of San Angelo, the vast farming area grows mainly cotton, milo and wheat. The farmers are mostly of German, Czech, and Bohemian descent, most all of whom are exceptionally frugal and darn good traders. Doing business with these guys has been an eternal challenge for all farm equipment dealers. Joe was provably good at negotiating with this thrifty bunch and was a friend to one and all.

Back in the days when that particular dealership was situated on the old parade grounds of Fort Concho in the middle of town, Joe's show lot was always overcrowded with new and used machinery of various kinds. I stopped there often for parts and supplies.

For several months, right by the main entrance to the yard sat an old Minneapolis-Moline tractor Joe had acquired in some trade. Not only was it probably 20-or-more-years-old, it showed evidence of a harsh life. I don't remember if it had an hour-meter to record its time of use, but if so, it would have rolled over to zero several times. The tractor sat there by the gate, unsold for months, drawing not even a look from any of the scores of farmers who frequented the dealership to pick up parts for their John Deere equipment.

Finally one day, I happened by that store on some mission, and to my great surprise, the old MM tractor was gone. I almost had to look around to see if I was where I thought I was. Upon entering the showroom, I quickly found Joe and asked him about the disappearance of the old Moline tractor.

"I sold it," Joe said matter-of-factly.

"SOLD IT?" I was incredulous. I couldn't believe the news. I pressed for details. "How in the world," I asked, "did you get that feat done? Who would want the thing?" I had always imagined that Joe would finally sell the old heap of rust to a scrap dealer.

And then I came at Joe with the most important question of all. "How did you ever find a buyer for that old tractor?"

Joe had a ready answer. "Remember that verse in the Bible, Skipper?"

Huh? What's he talking about? I was mystified. "What verse is that?"

"The one that says," Joe continued with a smile, "I saw he was a stranger, and I took him in."

The Offer

Prices for horses these days have changed so much I can barely keep up with trends. When I was most active in horse activities 40-50 years ago, a fair-to-middling ranch horse with some potential to make a roping horse might fetch $500-$750. A decent roping horse could be found for $1,250-$1,500. Tip-top roping horses cost $2,500. Every now and then, you'd hear of one that brought $3,500, but horses of that caliber were few and far between.

On one memorable occasion in the Brady rodeo arena after the performance, Marvin Cantrell was warming up a nice-looking horse before the roping slack commenced. Marvin, a well-known and successful roper, was also a consummate horse trader. Any animal he rode was always for sale. And boy-howdy, could Marvin ride a horse. Being a big guy, with exceptionally large, strong hands, he could hold the bridle's reins with the greatest of ease and apply subtle strength to the bit in the horse's mouth. He could make an ordinary horse look half-again better than he really was. No, maybe twice as good.

As Marvin put a well-muscled bay horse through several "roll-back-over-his-hocks" turns along a fence, a nearby spectator watched the show. The witness considered himself to be a world-class horse trader with an eye for potential in a prospect, and maybe he had just found a good'un. The bay gelding clearly handled with ease and was surely broke. At least he was with Marvin on his back.

Finally, the haughty buyer shouted at Marvin: "What will you take for that bay horse, mister?"

Sensing a potential trade, Marvin abandoned his reining lessons and rode over to the possible buyer standing by the bucking chutes. As he pulled up to a stop right in front of the guy, he said matter-of-factly, "I'll take $1,250 for him."

The clever buyer thought he knew something about trading, so without beating around the bush, he countered with an offer he considered to be ridiculously low. "I'll give," he said condescendingly, "$350." His intent, of course, was to intimidate Marvin and to start a negotiation of some kind.

Marvin stepped easily off the pony and handed him the reins, saying: "I don't know within $900 what a horse is worth. Sold. You just bought yourself a horse."

Imagine the horror felt by the new owner of the bay. He could only wonder about the stupendous hole in the horse that was bound to surface sooner or later.

In doing research for this book, I talked to Clayton Friend. He remembered an exact duplicate to the story above which happened at the livestock auction in Lubbock back when he and I were students at Tech. The only difference was the two prices. Clayton said an offer of $75 was immediately accepted for a horse that was priced only moments before at $350.

In both cases, the buyers were about to get the surprise of their lives. They surely, positively, unquestionably had not acquired bargains. Horse traders, despite their claims otherwise, don't offer steals.

Remember the lessons above. It is dangerous to say unequivocally, "I'll give $\_\_\_\_\_$." It is much safer to ask, "Would you take $_____$?" If the seller says "yes", you can get yourself out of the trap by replying, "Well, I was just wondering." That "I'll give $_____$" is a solid offer that is immediately binding on the buyer.

The old adage "Let the Buyer Beware" gains its credibility because of the inherent truth contained therein.

The Chevrolet Suburban

Sometime back in the 1980s, I was doing some economic calculations regarding car trades. My yellow pad full of arithmetic seemed to tell me that trading off a Chevrolet Suburban after only one year of use made good economic sense. I would be unable to recreate those figures now and the assumptions I used then are not important to the story anyway. The fact is that I swapped a one-year-old vehicle in on a brand new one after only a year of ownership.

My go-to man at Mustang Chevrolet was Joel Harris. As I recall the details, Joel was actually in charge of their fleet sales, but because we were old friends and because I dreaded dealing with a stranger, I sought out Joel when I arrived at the dealership. I explained my plan to him. Joel was delighted to help and found his printout listing their current inventory of new Suburban's. As his finger scrolled down the page, finally he found one he judged would meet my needs. He began the description by noting the motor size, the interior, and the various add-ons were more or less similar to the one I was trading back.

Finally, he found the color. "Oh good, Skipper," he praised. "You'll love the color. It is 'Desert Sand', one of our new colors this year. It is perfect for a rancher like you who drives frequently on dirt roads. That 'Desert Sand' is pretty, too. I know you will really, really like it."

Sure enough, when we found the vehicle out on their show lot, I did like it. It was perfect and for sure, I did like that "Desert Sand" color. Joel was right. Indeed, it was just what a country boy would need. We made the trade, and I left happy. Luxuriating in that new-car smell will do that to you.

A year later I returned for another trade with Joel. It was to be the third trial of my plan of trading after only 12 months. In those days, the body style of the Suburban's changed hardly at all. The newer models looked almost identical to the previous ones. And most all were equipped virtually alike. This process shouldn't take very long.

I quickly found Joel at his station on the second floor. His desk was covered with paperwork and as usual, he was busy. This time, I didn't have to review my plan – he pretty much remembered the details. All I wanted was a new car, equipped with all the standard accessories, more or less like I had purchased last year. Once again, Joel searched his data base to see what they might have in stock. Sure enough, they had one. Being super-busy with his fleet deals at the time, he told me where it was out on the lot. I went for a look-see and returned to Joel's desk to finalize the process.

Joel reached for his pad on which car deals are figured. He began writing up the order. When he got to the part about my trade-in, he started entering all the pertinent data. One of the lines asked for the color of the trade-in. At this request, Joel had to pause momentarily. He hadn't seen my "Desert Sand" parked outside, and he was trying to remember what he had sold me the year before.

Somewhat absent-mindedly, he finally had to ask, "Skipper, what was the color of that Suburban you bought last year?"

But before I could get the words "Desert Sand" out of my mouth, Joel suddenly had a brain-flash.

"Oh, that's right. I remember now."

This time, remember, he was trading back for the vehicle and was therefore "the buyer." He was calculating the trade-in value I would be getting.

"You bought that old mustard-colored Suburban last year."

Horse traders (a.k.a. car dealers) describe the exact same color differently depending on whether they are the sellers or the buyers.

That third trade ended my plan. I kept the last one and nearly wore it out. Buying "Desert Sand" and selling "Old Mustard" was a good lesson.

Roping Horses

During my more-or-less 10-year career roping calves, I probably never owned more than a dozen horses. Any horse I acquired was kept and used for my own selfish purposes until, for whatever reason, that horse no longer fit the program.

When a rookie is learning to rope calves, it takes a special horse to help him through that phase. The best horses for this specific duty are the older, experienced veterans who do just about the same thing every run. Finding a good, old, solid horse is more difficult than you might imagine. Often, by the time they are qualified to meet the standards, they are too stove-up for much use. After suffering through a couple of less-than-ideal learner horses, I finally acquired "Chubby." He was about 18 years old at the time and reasonably sound for his age. On his back, I began to master the craft of roping. Old Chubby was solid as a rock and did the exact same thing every time. Interestingly enough, the guy who trained him as a young horse, Lyn Griffin from Eldorado, told me that Chubby, in his youth, was a near-outlaw. Dan revealed he had hell ever breaking him, which was hard to imagine because with me, he was as gentle as a lamb.

I probably did my best roping when I began using "Rubber Gut," a blood-bay ranch pony that the horse trader, Walter Duke, had found over near Ballinger. No doubt, Rubber Gut never had spent much time in a roping arena until I bought him – he had been used solely for pasture roping back during the horrible days when screwworms plagued the West Texas ranch country. In the 1950s, many horses were hauled in the back of a pickup fitted with "stock racks" welded on the sides. Old Rubber Gut would readily jump right into the bed of a pickup if encouraged to do so. You won't find such horses these days. Walter Duke said his unusual name came from the fact that the old horse would eat absolutely anything. His particular favorite was watermelons.

After college, and as my interest in roping increased, my best roping buddy soon became Hal Churchill. Hal had moved to San Angelo from the Houston area. His new job was to report the livestock prices at our local market, Producers Livestock Auction. Hal had roped calves for years and had competed at many of the large professional rodeos all across the nation. For an eager student like me, Hal was a good professor.

But Hal's keenest interest was roping horses. He was a master trainer. Rarely did he ever own more than two horses at a time – one to haul to the ropings and another young horse on which he trained. Hal would never admit it, but he was more interested in trading horses than anything. Nothing tickled him more than selling a horse.

There are many factors which determine the value of a roping horse. Quite obviously, the higher the price for the horse, the more skills he (she) would (or should) have. Desired traits were several: The horse needed to be calm and attentive while in the box so the roper could get a good start on his run. Then, he needed speed from a standing start to quickly overtake the fleeing calf. Next, you wanted a sudden, hard stop when the calf was roped to jerk him down and take some of the fight out of him. "Rope-working" skills were always a plus if the horse would back up, thereby drawing the calf toward the approaching roper now on the ground. Lastly, the horse should be just as good at a rodeo with all the distractions and noises as he is in a practice pen at home.

Hal Churchill

Horses might excel at one or two of these traits but be deficient, or marginal in the others. The sum of the horse's attributes would govern the price of the animal. In this regard, Hal made an important observation. If your present horse lacked speed and you were looking to replace him, you would focus only on that sole attribute in a potential future prospect and neglect all the other factors. Must have something to do with Human Nature. The exploitation of this fact has been mastered by horse traders the world over.

When I would attend the weekly auction in my quest to buy roping calves, Hal was always available to drink coffee and to talk roping horses. And whichever roping horse he happened to own at the time was for sale, although this fact was always carefully hidden. Hal would start his discourse on his current horse by stating matter-of-factly that he now had "THE BEST HORSE HE'D EVER OWNED." Bragging endlessly on the horse's strongest attributes, he would recount example after example. I would sit there amazed, wondering if finally, finally, Hal now owned a "perfect" horse. Of course, he never mentioned any shortcomings, keeping those cards close to his vest. After listening week after week to his bragging, I would conclude that, finally, here was a horse that Hal would never sell. He owned, according to what I was hearing, what he always dreamed of in a horse. Just like me, Hal was finally ready to keep his "best" horse forever. Good for him and to hell with that endless swapping.

Being the slow learner than I am, it took a mighty long time for me to realize that Hal was using me mainly to practice his sales pitch. But I was a good listener and an eager audience. That only encouraged Hal to make greater claims about the subject at hand. Other ropers, too, joined the audience for Hal's mighty claims about his current horse. Hindsight tells me that Hall was baiting lots of hooks in hopes of getting a bite.

Then, all of a sudden and from out of nowhere when we would meet at the coffee shop in the auction, Hal would announce proudly that he had sold the very horse that had been No. 1 on his Hit Parade the past few months. Time after time, I couldn't believe what I was hearing. I thought Hal said this was "THE BEST" one ever, so why would he sell such an animal? In fact, over the years, he did indeed sell some good ones that wound up on the professional circuit.

Almost immediately after a sale, Hal would begin telling me about a prospect he had bought somewhere recently. Slowly but surely, he would inevitably begin to brag on the new acquisition over the coming weeks. It was as if he led a double life, horse trainer and horse trader.

Toad Tucker recalls a time when he ran into Hal at the auction. In his youth, Toad rodeoed a bit but never roped calves or steers in competition. Toad had little interest in the sport except for maybe a friendly bet on the big match roping in the fall. But being the only sounding board available at the time, Toad was subjected to Hal and those extravagant claims about his current horse. Toad graciously listened as Hal went on and on detailing skill after skill possessed by "THE BEST HORSE" Hal had ever owned. Toad was impressed. He'd never heard of such a horse. This one had to be the perfect roping horse. At least Toad had never heard of one any better.

Finally, after about 30 minutes into the sermon, Hal popped the question to Toad that had been on his mind when he started. Hal knew that few people know more cowboys than Toad Tucker does. It never hurts to spread the word.

"Toad," Hal asked confidentially, "What do you suppose a horse like mine ought to be worth?"

Lesson: when you hear endless bragging on a horse, a gun, a boat, a vehicle, or whatever – be careful.

The Hippie's Horse

Kenneth Crain is a cowboy's cowboy. He looks the part. He acts the part. He talks the part.

I had seen Kenneth here and there before I ever got to know him. He was impossible to miss. His huge black hat with its 5-inch brim and Hopalong Cassidy crown was a dead giveaway. Combine that with his pant legs tucked into his high-topped, high-heeled boots and throw in the homemade pocket knife pouch on his belt around his tight-fitting Wranglers, and you had someone with the appearance of a genuine cowboy. He usually had a bandana around his neck, too.

Kenneth Crain

The appearance didn't lie. Kenneth's occupation at the time was "Day-Working Cowboy." Anyone who hires out himself and his horse for temporary work on area ranches will inevitably find more "true-west" experiences than can be found in a decade's worth of cowboy magazines and songs. Kenneth can talk for hours about his many adventures with eccentric ranch and livestock owners. It's a wonder he survived that part of his life.

I finally got better acquainted with Kenneth when he was hired to be the ranch foreman on the Wardlaw Brothers Ranch to the north of my place. For a few years, we conducted our Adobe Lodge hunts there, and it wasn't long before Kenneth took time to guide for us every now and then. Kenneth was always a huge hit with any of his hunters.

Somehow, they sensed they were in the presence of a genuine character.

Kenneth has a wealth of stories about cowboying, ranching and hunting. When the subject of horse trading arises, as it has in this chapter, Kenneth could chime in with a dandy tale of his own.

Kenneth had consigned a horse to an area auction. The pony sold early in the sale, and Kenneth admitted that the horse brought more than he had thought it would, which is always a pleasant surprise when you are selling a horse at an auction, come to think of it. So he was in a good mood as he watched the rest of the auction unfold, drinking a little beer along the way in celebration of his good fortune.

Finally, all but one of the horses had been sold. Most of the crowd had dispersed. Only Kenneth, sitting on the top row of the stands, and a few hardcore horse traders remained. The sorrel horse being offered appeared to be maybe a three-year-old and was ridden bareback into the sales ring by his owner, a hippie. Or, at least, he looked like a hippie with his head band, his pony tail, his flowery shirt and his sandals. Yep, he was a hippie all right.

The auctioneer started the deal by asking for a bid of $100. His voice rolled on and on, imploring anyone, anywhere to make a bid. Only a $100, folks. Who'll give a 100? How about a 100? Just a $100 dollar bill. The chant of a good auctioneer will have an almost musical quality, and this particular practitioner was a good one. You'd never get tired of his melody. And it was easy to follow his quest for a bid. But try as he might, he could never get that initial $100 offer.

The hippy continued to ride his horse from one end of the small sales ring to the other. The horse seemed to be gentle, and he did turn around fairly well. But still there were no bids. The bored horse traders left in the auction barn had no interest and sat on their hands. Meanwhile, the diligent auctioneer droned on and on, begging for a bid – any bid would do.

Good grief, thought Kenneth, in this day and time, almost any horse ought to be worth $100. Finally, he could stand it no more. He raised his hand and almost simultaneously, the auctioneer took Kenneth's $100 bid and sold out. The sale was over. Kenneth was shocked and somewhat sobered by the quickness of the deal.

Kenneth wandered outside to the trailer area, still berating himself for his impulsive act. He came with a horse; now he was returning home with a horse. His feed bill would see no decline.

It didn't take much of an effort to spot the hippie's rig. A rattletrap trailer was drawn behind a colorful van. A nearby woman busied herself getting things organized for their departure. No doubt, with her Earth Mother dress, her string of beads, and her hair plaited into two long pigtails, she was the hippie's wife. Or whatever that relationship is called in Hippiedom.

Kenneth, in his traditional cowboy garb, approached the woman and made a simple announcement:

"Well," he noted, "I just bought your horse."

"Oh, that's wonderful," gushed the woman. "You will just love 'Prince'. He is a most noble animal. We just hated to sell him, but there was no way to continue keeping him as we move into the next realm of our shared existence. You will be so lucky to bond with Prince as we have. I'm sure he will grow to love you as he has us."

All the psycho-babble went right over Kenneth's head. He didn't know what the crazed woman was talking about. But he did hope for some clue about the horse, so he asked, as any cowboy would:

"Will he look at a cow?" This legitimate question would be the first thing on a cowboy's list of desirable traits.

"Oh, no, no," assured the hippie-lady. "You don't have to worry about that."

Kenneth squinted his eyes and cocked his head a bit to be sure he would not miss a word of her explanation. He was beginning to understand that she didn't quite speak his language.

She continued with her guarantee. "We took him to the vet last year and HAD HIM FIXED. He won't be bothering any of your cattle."

Terry Ford

Back before the steep decline in livestock numbers in West Texas which began sometime in the 1980s, ranch horses were abundant across the land. It takes plenty of hands on horses to gather livestock in large, brushy pastures. So with horses being just another cog in the machinery of a ranching operation, horse traders were an integral part of the overall scene. One of the best was Terry Ford.

Terry Ford

Terry lived and worked out of Mertzon, just west of San Angelo. In all directions from that town, large sheep, goat and cattle operations could be found. If you needed a horse or two or three, Terry could be counted on to find just what you needed at a price you wanted to pay. Conversely, if you owned a horse or two or three that might be old, or permanently crippled or no longer needed, Terry was a ready buyer for whatever you happened to have. He would obligingly show up at your place with his long gooseneck trailer and save you the trouble of hauling the horses yourself. Honest to a fault, Terry was a good horseman and a good judge of horseflesh. Being full of stories and good cheer, Terry had a wide base of customers.

But as the relentless decline in livestock numbers continued year after year, the number of ranch horses declined as well, exacerbated by droughts and the inexorable move from productive ranching to recreational uses of land such as hunting. The consequence of this paradigm shift was a major blow to Terry's horse-trading activities. Year-by-year, there were fewer horses in the ranch country and fewer trades he could make. The resourceful Terry finally took a job as an insurance adjuster working hail storms and hurricane disasters. And obviously, this activity took him away from the San Angelo area for months at a time.

The West Texas horse trader got exposed to all kinds of wonders not seen around home. Terry found himself in the Chicago area working a storm of some kind. He had always heard about the Chicago Cubs and vowed to see a game while he was in the area. In the reporting of his experience that day, Terry said he'd never seen so many people. "It looked like," he remarked memorably, "that someone had kicked the top off a fire ant bed." If that's not a perfectly descriptive phrase, I've never heard one.

He continued to trade a few horses when he returned home, and being addicted to team roping, he always kept a few horses around for his own personal use whenever he could find the time. This change for Terry came sometime during the first decade of the 21st century.

Horse Trading

It was along about then, as most everyone remembers, that credit was easy and cheap. A local radio advertisement was repeated relentlessly all the live-long day. The ad said:

"If you have a job and $200, you can get a new car."

The radio station we all listened to must have played the ad every five minutes. I never got so sick of hearing anything in my life. I vowed to never buy a vehicle from that particular dealership.

One day, I happened to run into Terry Ford who had returned home from one of his adjusting trips. He asked if I had been listening to the radio. Yep, from time to time – why do you ask?

Terry wondered if I had heard that amazing automobile advertisement which promised you a new car if you had a job and $200?

"Good grief," I answered, "I'm sick of that thing. They play it over and over all day long. I can almost quote you every word of that dialog." I continued my harangue and finally ran out of breath.

A quizzical look came on Terry's face as he wondered aloud, "I don't understand that ad at all."

I was incredulous at that statement. Being the veteran horse trader that he was, Terry surely ought to be able to understand the proposal offered by the dealership. It could not have been more straightforward. But maybe I was missing something?

"What's not to understand about that ad, Terry?" I still couldn't believe that an experienced swapper and trader might be confused.

"Here's my question, Skipper," Terry confided with a twinkle in his eye. "If you have $200, why would you want a job?"

The Horse Trade

For those who might only occasionally buy or sell a horse, here is a tale that might be of benefit on some future deal. Since all the various participants are still alive and kicking, names, dates, towns and other identity clues shall remain cloudy. And that includes the horse to be introduced shortly. Maybe he still lives or maybe he has already met an untimely end.

The saga which follows was told to me by a master of the craft of storytelling. But if I revealed his name, all the mysteries listed above would be revealed. Truthfully, I would love to give him proper credit.

A rancher, let's call him Roy, was schooling a young horse in his corral one day. Roy, a fair hand with a horse, had only recently acquired the pony from Hank, another aficionado of good horse flesh. Roy was putting the horse through his paces, loping in figure eights in the large pen where he habitually trained his young horses.

As he continued with the schooling, up to his ranch corrals drove the local horse trader, Sam, unannounced as always. You never knew when Sam might show up but being gregarious and extroverted as he was, it was a treat to see him and he was always welcome. Roy and Sam had swapped horses for years. Roy might occasionally have something for sale, and Sam, being a trader, was always on the lookout for a likely prospect he could turn quickly to make a profit.

Sam watched the show from outside the corrals. The sorrel was probably about a four-year-old and appeared to be well-broken but not yet "finished" to the satisfaction of Roy. Roy had the horse well warmed up by now, and he was showing plenty of handle – spinning both ways along a fence. He would strike an easy lope and sit right on his butt when Roy gave him the clue to stop. The horse was beginning to sweat a bit from all the exertion, but he appeared calm as could be. Sam was impressed with what he was seeing.

Horse Trading

Because the two men had done plenty of horse business over the years, there was really no reason to beat around the bush. Each could read the other's mind. Roy pulled up on the reins and walked the sorrel to the fence to greet his visitor. After the howdy and the handshake, Sam complimented Roy on this new horse he was riding. Looks to be a good prospect, he observed honestly. Handles good and all that.

Yep. Yep. Roy remained non-committal, correctly suspecting that Sam had an interest. Sure enough, Sam finally came to his point.

Sam mentioned that he was looking for a roping prospect for a guy he knew in town. Had Roy, he wondered, ever tried to rope anything on the horse?

Nope, not much. Just trailed a goat around a pen a bit to get the horse used to the swinging lariat over his head. He was probably ready for more advanced work and might be just what Sam was seeking.

The conversation between the two continued in this vein until Sam finally popped the question. "What would it take to buy this horse?" he asked of Roy.

Roy cut to the chase and said without hesitation he wouldn't take a penny less than $1,500 for him. Sam and Roy had been down this trail many times over the years, and Sam, being the judge of people that he was, knew that Roy didn't like to haggle. In the interest of time, Sam quickly said, by golly, he believed the horse might be worth it, and by golly he'd just buy him. By golly. So the trade was made. Roy pulled his saddle off the horse, and Sam found a halter to replace Roy's bridle. The entire episode hadn't taken 10 minutes. Sam left with his new horse, and Roy retreated to his stable to find another horse to tutor for the remainder of the morning.

The next afternoon in town, a team roping practice was set to commence. Several of the town cowboys showed up after work to hone their skills. Sam arrived from his day's adventures, but he had taken care to bring along that new horse in his trailer. He had kept the horse overnight in his trading pens and continued to be pleased with his purchase. His potential prospect, Willy, as Sam had hoped, showed up for the practice session. Sam lost no time in showing the new horse to Willy and went into great detail about the attributes of the horse which he had seen just the day before.

"He's a dandy," Sam assured Willy. "He's well-broke and ready for you to start training. No doubt you are looking at your next great roping horse. No telling what you'll make out of him, but I'm betting he will be the best one you've had in years." Sam went on and on, painting a bright future for Willy and this new sorrel horse.

Willy knew that Sam knew a good horse when he saw one. So that was enough for him. He promptly asked Sam what the price of the horse might be. When Sam said $1,750 would buy him, Willy closed the deal on the spot. Thinking that the gain of $250 after just one day of ownership was a decent profit, Sam even threw in the $10 halter on the deal. They shook hands, and Sam departed, leaving Willy with his new horse.

Early the next morning, Willy's wife called Sam, distressed beyond belief. As Sam understood the story, Willy had saddled the horse after Sam's departure. So far, so good. But when Willy tried to mount him, and just as his leg passed over the rear of the saddle, the horse bolted backwards for several yards, reared up, and purposely fell over backward with Willy half astride the pony for the entire way. Result: Willy's leg got broken. Badly. She was at the hospital all night. What kind of a horse did you sell my husband, anyway? He almost got killed. That horse is a complete idiot. Willy might not be able to work for weeks now. What the hell are you going to do about this?

Sam assured the distraught woman that he would look into the deal, and he promised to contact her and her husband later in the day. After all, he said, they had been up all night and badly needed some rest. Besides, he needed time to think. What WAS he going to do about all this?

After several more attempts at consoling the poor wife, Sam bid her goodbye. Quickly now, he drove to Roy's distant ranch as fast as his truck would carry him. During the trip, he kept remembering every detail of the horse he had owned for such a brief time. Try as he might, he could recall nothing sinister about the horse. In fact, he seemed to be quite gentle.

Unsurprisingly, Roy had another horse saddled and was riding him in that large corral as Sam arrived. He skidded up to the fence in a cloud of dust and hollered for Roy to come quick.

Sam told Roy all about the accident and detailed the event of the horse bolting backwards with Willy not yet half in the saddle. Roy listened easily to the story without much alarm. In his mind, he could picture the scene. When Sam finally stopped his tirade, mainly to catch his breath, Roy noted quite frankly, "Yeah, that rascal did that to me several times."

"He did?" Sam was incredulous. "Set backwards with you, too? Several times, you say?"

"Yep," Roy went on. "Whenever he is fresh, and whenever you tighten the cinch, that dude will throw a fit. He'll run backwards and fall right smack-back over his hocks, banging his head on the ground. But not every time. Sometimes he will wait to pull that little trick until just at that moment when you try to get on him. Of course, I always just stepped aside and let the idiot go."

Sam couldn't believe what he was hearing.

Roy went on with his history lesson. "But after he pulls that stunt, you can finally get on him and he rides out fine.

Just like you saw yesterday morning. He's really a pretty good horse once you understand that little quirk about him."

Sam couldn't believe his ears. Roy had never misrepresented a horse before.

"Gosh, Roy," Sam said in wonderment. "Why didn't you tell me about all this yesterday before I bought the horse?"

Roy had a ready and totally honest answer.

"Well, Sam," he went on easily, "remember I told you I had bought the horse a few weeks ago from Hank Jones. Hank never told me about this bad habit, so I THOUGHT IT WAS A SECRET."

Tales Galore

Chain Saws

Years ago when friends would ask if they could come cut some mesquite firewood at my ranch, I was always agreeable.

From a distance, I could hear their chain saw screaming away for a few minutes. Then – total silence. When I would go out in the pasture to visit the work scene, invariably the saw was broken into several mysterious parts. The owner, with tools scattered all across the tailgate of his truck, would be attempting to repair something or other.

Being the world's worst mechanic, I knew I could never keep one of the things running long enough to harvest a wheelbarrow full of wood. I was at least 30 years into my ranching career before I ever owned a chain saw. Never needed one. After large portions of the ranch were root-plowed, all those old dead limbs had cured for years. It was easy enough to gather firewood just driving through the area.

But after watching our legendary camp cook, Pon Lawdermilk, cut perfect "steak wood" from old, dead, gray mesquite, I decided maybe, after all, I ought to own one of the things. So I purchased a lightweight model perfect for trimming limbs as much as 12 inches thick. I set to work clearing a fence line where ancient, giant mesquites had grown out over a fence next to a field.

Yes, I did have a little trouble with the thing as I began to learn its peculiarities. But super-mechanic David Ocker at the Dixie Hardware store in Ballinger was a wealth of information about the device. Once he showed me how to start it when it was cold, and then how to start it again once it was warm, I had little more trouble and finally wore it out. That little Stihl was a good saw.

Several summers, my wife, Jeri, and I went to visit my oldest stepson, Jim and his wife, Jennifer, on the Gander Ranch, which they managed in eastern Oregon for several years. The Gander Ranch was a spectacularly beautiful place about 25 miles southwest of John Day and had a harvestable stand of Ponderosa pines.

One summer, a pair of honest-to-goodness lumberjacks was on site falling trees. (They don't refer to the process as "cutting down trees.") You talk about chain saws – mercy – those two guys used giant devices with 32" bars and could drop a 100-foot tree on a distant beer can if they had they chosen to do so. Most certainly, that was work for professionals. I could easily see the danger from "falling" trees.

One used a Stihl; the other had a Husqvarna. I took photo after photo. During their brief coffee break while they filled up with gasoline and oil, and just to be a bit ornery, I ask the two amigos which brand of saw was the best. You never heard such an argument in your life. It was a confrontation akin to a Democrat and a Republican on a Sunday morning talk show.

Amazingly, the two chain saws I now own sit for months unused in the barn, but when pressed into service, they are ready to go. And I have created a couple of new maxims that would be readily agreed-to by all wood cutters:

"Happiness is a sharp blade on a chain saw."
"Happiness is a chain saw that starts."

The old joke about the little boy who swapped his lawnmower to a preacher for a bicycle comes to mind when talking about chain saws that won't start.

The preacher needed the lawnmower; the boy wanted that preacher's bicycle. A week or so later, the boy rode his new bicycle down the sidewalk and spotted the old minister trying without success to start the mower. He stopped to offer the preacher some sage advice. "You'll have to give that thing a good cussing before it will start," he counseled.

Indignantly, the man of the cloth replied, "Son, it's been over 40 years since curse words passed out of my lips."

The boy knew just what to do. "Keep pulling on that rope a while, mister. All of them will come back to you."

Having experienced that same frustration of a saw which refuses to start when your work crew is assembled and everything is set to go, I can appreciate the following story I heard in a San Angelo store where I buy parts. More or less, here is the dialog between the customer and the clerk:

Customer: "I'm here to buy a new chain saw."

Clerk: "I'm sure we can help you. What model do you need?"

Customer: "I guess I want one just like my old one. It won't start anymore."

Clerk: "I'll be happy to sell you a new one. But about that old saw, maybe we could repair it instead."

Customer: "I don't think you could fix it."

Clerk: "Why?"

Customer: "It's full of water."

Clerk: "Full of water, eh? For Pete's sake, how did it get full of water?"

Customer: "It's halfway out in the middle of the river on my place."

Clerk: "How in the world did it get halfway out in the middle of the river?"

Customer: "I couldn't throw it any farther than that."

Great Advice

Shoeing horses is about the hardest work I've ever done. I'm not particularly good at it, and it takes me a full hour to complete the task that a professional can do much better in about 20 minutes. But for a variety of reasons, back in the days when I owned several horses, I did all the shoeing and trimming.

Once you get the horse's foot properly shaped for the horseshoe, it is time to affix the shoe to the pad of the foot with nails. A horseshoe nail is pointed and beveled to exit the hoof about an inch or so from the bottom of the horse's foot. If you have pointed it correctly, that does it.

You hold the horse's front foot between your legs. When that nail is placed through the hole in the horseshoe and hammered through the wall of the hoof, that nail is like a lethal weapon until you can bend it and break it off. A horseshoer will take care to do just that as soon as each nail is driven home. The process won't take but a second or two, but you don't dare leave that nail exposed and unbent or broken. Reason: If the horse happens to jerk his foot away from you at that very moment, the exposed long, sharp nail can do mighty damage if it finds some of your flesh.

One of those nails got me one time. I was working on a hammer-headed ranch horse. Just at the right instant, the devil jerked his foot away in a violent manner. The exposed nail ripped a couple of "v" shaped chunks out of the bottom of my little finger. Blood spurted as I yelped in pain and cussed the worthless nag for all he was worth. And at that point, I didn't consider him to be worth much at all.

I rushed to the other end of the barn where the sink was. Running a slow stream of water over my finger, I could now see the extent of the damage. Maybe I ought to go to town and let someone sew it up? Maybe get a tetanus shot, too? How long had it been since my last one?

So with my finger wrapped in a towel to soak up all the blood, I made the 30-minute trip to the "Doctor's Clinic." Before too long, I was ushered in to see Dr. Gus Eckhardt. It didn't take long for him to clean the area, deaden it (thank goodness) and put a half-dozen nifty stitches here and there in both cuts. Until that painkiller wore off after a while, I was good as new.

But what made that particular doctor's visit memorable and super valuable was the advice Dr. Gus gave me as I left. His instruction went something like this:

"Now Skipper, you probably don't realize it, but that is a very dangerous wound. You will have to be extra careful to be sure infection doesn't set in. So for that reason, I have to insist that you don't do any dishes or carry out any garbage for five years."

With advice like that, it is no wonder Dr. Gus Eckhardt was one of our town's most popular surgeons. And he practiced medicine well into his 90s, too. At this writing, he is less than a year away from his 100th birthday.

Tales Galore: And a Whole Lot More

The Irrigation Pump

When our Middle Concho River was a more reliable source of water than it is now, I tried my hand at irrigating crops. I bought a trailer-mounted portable pump equipped with a 292-cubic-inch Chevrolet six-cylinder engine which ran on propane. It was an efficient rig. I could move it from place to place along the river. Water extracted from the river would flow through 10-inch aluminum pipes away from the river to various ditches which carried the precious fluid here and there in the fields.

Once one area of a field was thoroughly wet, the pump and pipe would be relocated to a different area in the field. Unfortunately, there weren't all that many handy places to station the pump. The contraption had to be right next to the bank of the river so that the large intake pipe could be submerged in the river. All those chores were lots of work, and I doubt I ever produced enough additional crops to cover my expenses, much less my labor. But that enlightenment was slow to come. For a couple of years, I did the best I could and worked my tail off.

One memorable time, in moving the pump to a brand new location, the hitch pin which tied the pump rig to my tractor came loose and the entire shebang rolled down the slope and disappeared into the river. Needless to say, it was a monumental effort to extract the thing. Once back on dry ground, I pulled the pump trailer to a mechanic I knew in town. Bill Sanders out on Bell Street was just the guy to put things right with that engine which had been submerged overnight.

About a week later, Bill called to announce that the pump was ready to go. He had drained all the water out of the engine, replaced the oil and had the thing running pretty darn good, he said.

Giving up on that dangerous site for the pump, I found a more likely place down river and took a day or so to get everything hooked up and ready to pump. The fuel source for the engine was a 250-gallon propane tank, similarly mounted on another set of wheels situated nearby. Propane was transferred to the Chevy engine via a long copper tube. The flow pipe for the river water coming away from the pump had to climb a fairly steep slope to finally get the water out to the ditch in the nearby field. The entire scene would have done credit to Rube Goldberg and some of his complicated drawings.

But finally, it was all ready and the engine was started one nice spring morning. The water was flowing easily into the ditch to the far end of the field where it was being used. I scrambled up the hill and ran down the ditch just to be sure everything was in order. It was. The field was getting wet. Finally, all was right with the world. Nothing warms the heart of a West Texas farmer more than the sight of water flowing across his crop land.

After about 30 minutes of such reverie, things were about to change in a big way.

Alarm bells started ringing when the ranch hand who had been left down by the river near the engine to complete some task came running as fast as he could. He was jabbering more Spanish than I could understand. His excitement knew no bounds, and he waved for me to come quick. I couldn't imagine what caused his alarm.

Once back on the top of the slope next to the river, I was horrified to see that the old Middle Concho was flooding. A rise on the river had come from nowhere, and water was rising around my engine and propane tank. I had seen a large cloud out in the west the previous afternoon but thought nothing of it. All that was miles and miles away. Our sky at home had been perfectly clear. No doubt, that cloud had been the source of this unexpected deluge. Now what?

The flood water was about even with the bottom of the engine which, surprisingly, was still running. But more water was on the way, and you could actually see it rising bit by bit. Quickly, we secured a chain to the tongue of the engine and got it hitched to the pickup. Water was now beginning to float the propane trailer but because it was tethered to the engine with that flimsy copper pipe, the trailer bobbed and floated just like a cork on a fishing pole. Rising water soon killed the engine, and somehow, the pickup pulled it up out of the water. The propane tank, now freed when the fuel line broke, went sailing down the river. If you could have mounted the thing, it would have been an awesome ride.

Grabbing an old lariat out of the bed of the pickup, I raced down the river to a narrow spot about a quarter-mile distant. When the tank floated by, I made the best catch of my roping career and tied the rig off to a nearby pecan tree. It could be properly relocated after the river returned to normal.

Once the disaster was finally over, I had to take the pump and engine back to Bill Sanders yet again. What he told me that day was a classic. He said earnestly:

"Skipper, I'm not sure how long I can keep this engine running if you keep baptizing it every week."

Prude Ranch

Prude Ranch is primarily a kid's camp, located a few miles up Limpia Creek just west of Fort Davis out in the Davis Mountains of far West Texas.

For many decades now, visiting youngsters have ridden horses, swum, shot arrows and .22s, hiked, and experienced that beautiful scenery in the Davis Mountains. Even one of our high school groups went there back in the 1950s. So it has been there a long, long time – a tribute to their outstanding program and well-deserved reputation.

My wife, Jeri, thought her two boys, despite having access to all manner of outdoor adventures on my ranch, would benefit from attending Prude Ranch after having attended a small, church-sponsored school for their first six years. The boys would gain valuable social skills for their advancement into the higher grades in the public school system. It worked. We felt that both boys benefited from their experience as campers at Prude Ranch.

Some years later, Randy, the younger of the two, attended college at Sul Ross in nearby Alpine during the mid-1990s. One summer, he found a job working as a counselor at Prude Ranch. It was to be yet another beneficial time for him as he learned to work with the kids.

As each new group of campers arrived at the ranch for their week or two-week stay, the boys and the girls would be divided into groups to fit the various dormitory units. On one particular rotation, Randy and his fellow counselor were assigned a group of 11-year-old boys. For many of them, it was their first real adventure away from home and parents. And having been deposited in the vast Chihuahuan Desert, everything they saw was new to them.

The mischievous counselors would caution their impressionable campers that Indians still roamed the surrounding hills, and everyone would have to be on their

RANDY HOLT

guard for attacks by the savages. That first night, as everyone was finally getting to bed, the counselors kept up their dialog about the Redskins. Similar misinformation was being spread throughout the other dorms by the other leaders.

About thirty minutes after lights-out, a pre-arranged signal was given. An Indian war party was attacking. "War drums" (were counselors beating them?) were providing a terrifying noise. Everyone could hear attackers coming as the leaders rushed to get their campers out of bed and away from the dorm. The screams of the terrified kids only added to the confusion. Everyone was rushed "to safety," with the Indians drawing ever closer.

Once outside at the rendezvous location, Randy and his fellow counselor counted heads and found one of their group missing. Randy returned immediately with a flashlight to search the dormitory. He found the trembling 11-year-old hiding beneath his bunk. He was paralyzed with fear, shivering uncontrollably.

"Come on. Quick," Randy ordered. "The Indians are nearly here." The boy wouldn't budge. Then, he really got Randy's attention when he said:

"Oh, no. The Indians are coming to kill me. I won't live through the night. And I haven't even had sex yet."

My, how times have changed. Who would have ever thought that a boy of that age would make such a statement?

6666 Country

In the late 1990s, we began offering a few mule deer hunts on the Felix River Ranch southwest of Roswell, N.M. Adobe

Lodge activities there were managed by Jim Schwarz, who had guided for us a number of years and was quite familiar with our program. Because many of our hunters seemed to be interested in hunting mulies, I began to wonder about hunting that species up in the Texas panhandle, as well. In early January, 2000, the search for a likely place began.

Toad Tucker knows more people than anyone I ever met. Once I outlined my plan to him, Toad suggested I contact a veterinarian he knew, Dr. Pat Crouch, up at Canadian in the northeastern part of the Panhandle. Toad correctly surmised that few people would know more ranchers than a vet. So I called Dr. Crouch and made an appointment to meet with him the following week. Luckily, Toad even agreed to go on the trip.

Toad, Jim and I loaded up and headed north. With our destination being the eastern side of the panhandle, our route took us right through Guthrie, Texas, home of the legendary 6666 Ranch. I was driving with Toad sitting on the passenger side of the double-cab. Schwarz lounged in the back seat reading a book.

That big ranch country around Guthrie is spectacular. Miles and miles of pastureland as far as the eye can see, all of which is owned by the Sixes. On my few trips through the area, I always reflected on its history. The Comanche Indians kept early settlers at bay for decades. That prairie had been some of the winter range for the vast herds of buffalos. In that part of the world, cattlemen didn't make much headway in taking the land away from the Indians until after the Civil War.

As I drove along U.S. Highway 83, I couldn't quit thinking about the history of North Central Texas. Surely the rangeland had changed big-time since the days of the Indians. Who knows what the country looked like before the inexorable encroachment of mesquites and brush? I always wondered about such matters. Back in the days when the Indians were in charge and range fires burned unchecked for miles, what did all that country look like?

So as I drove along through the 6666 country, I just happened to mention to my companions the thoughts that were racing through my mind. Both Toad and Jim were cowboys at heart and both were well-read in the history of the Texas frontier.

"Wow", I mused. "Wouldn't it be something to see all this country back before the turn of the century?" I was trying to imagine that endless, open prairie those many years ago without a fence, a road, a windmill or a house in sight. I could imagine myself astride a good horse, trailing a bunch of cattle to the north.

Toad chimed in with an affirmation. "Yes sir. It surely would. No telling what it looked like back during the previous century." Toad, like me, had dreamed of big ranches and their large livestock operations.

For a while there, we were both lost in our own worlds, wondering about such a time.

Jim, sitting there in the back seat, had been listening to all our speculation. He brought both Toad and me back to hard reality when he noted:

"Good Gosh Awl-Mighty, you two," he observed. "'Back before the turn of the century' is what I keep hearing. You old cowboys are nuts. It's just the 10th of January, 2000. The country surely couldn't have changed all that much in the past two weeks."

Tales Galore

The Perfect Arrowhead

You just don't see too many flawless arrowheads. A few come close, but most are symmetrically imperfect in some way.

David Gonzales, our inimitable deer skinner and all-around hand at the hunting camp, found one on my ranch that was almost textbook. We had been hauling some old bricks to dump into a gully to halt erosion. As David was scattering the material, I returned to the barn for another load. Given a brief period of inactivity, David will invariably look for arrowheads or anything else he might find.

When I returned with yet another load to dump in the hole, David produced his find. It was so spectacular that I accused him of playing a trick – he had brought the treasure from his extensive collection at home and was trying to fool me.

Nope, asserted David. He claimed forcefully that he had found it only moments before my arrival.

No way, I protested. You are just playing a giant hoax on me.

No, sir, claimed David, and here's proof. He rolled up his sleeve to show me the goose bumps still on his arm.

That evidence was unassailable, I suppose. Who can produce goose bumps at will?

Taxidermist Henry Dusek obligingly visits our hunting camp to collect any deer heads for mounting. Henry has a good system. The hunters get to meet him in person, and Henry brings lots of photos to demonstrate the various

Henry Dusek

choices he offers for deer mounts. He can explain his entire program, the various costs of each example, possible dates of completion, and will answer a variety of questions each hunter might have.

One evening, Henry showed up at the lodge right on schedule, a bit before the pending arrival of the hunters from their afternoon's adventures. Henry had news.

"Did I tell you about the great arrowhead I found, Skipper?" Henry began.

"Nope, I hadn't heard you'd found a good one. What did it look like?"

"Oh, mercy, Me-OH-My," he continued, "It was absolutely perfect. Perfect in every way."

"Wow, Henry. How big was it? What did it look like? I'd love to see it sometime." It sounded as if he'd found a real treasure and, yes, I was a bit jealous.

"Look here. I'll show you just what a flawless point it is." Henry quickly grabbed a piece of paper in his briefcase and being left-handed, he began to draw an outline of his prize. Starting from the point of the flint, he started sketching one edge of the rock:

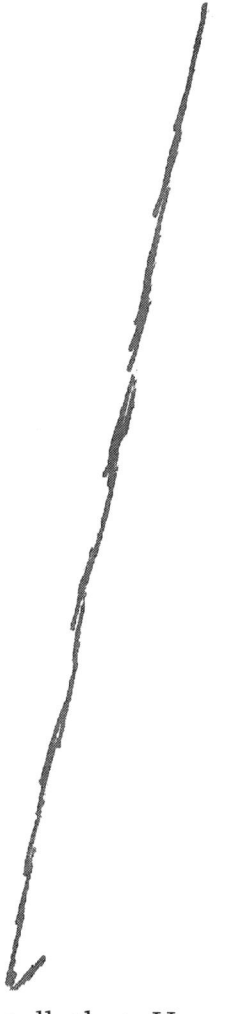

Already, I could tell that Henry had found an extra-large arrowhead. Most aren't anywhere close to that size. Scratching and scribbling with that left hand, Henry kept up a running dialog of just how the image was coming along. He began to describe the bottom and made careful twists and turns with that pencil of his:

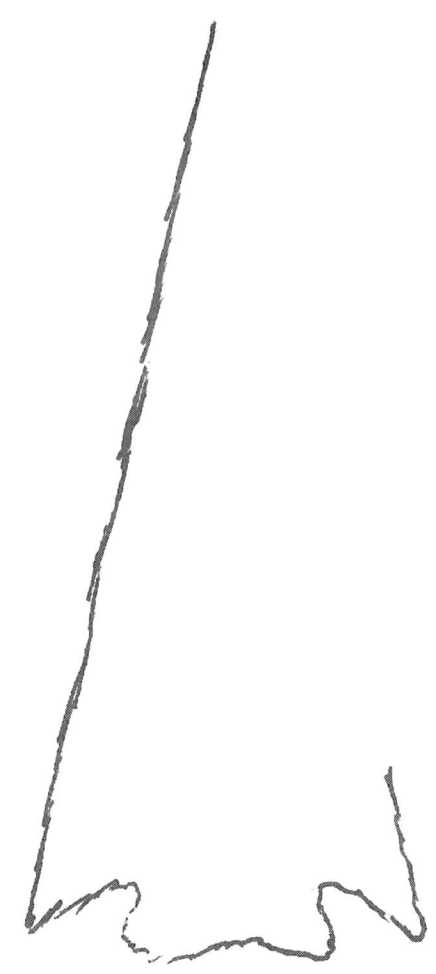

I was holding my breath. The arrowhead Henry was drawing was simply spectacular. That busy left hand could hardly keep up with the play-by-play he was recounting. He got more and more excited as he continued sketching. Finally, after an unbearably long time, his artistic creation had been completed to his satisfaction. It was nothing short of perfection, just as he had claimed.

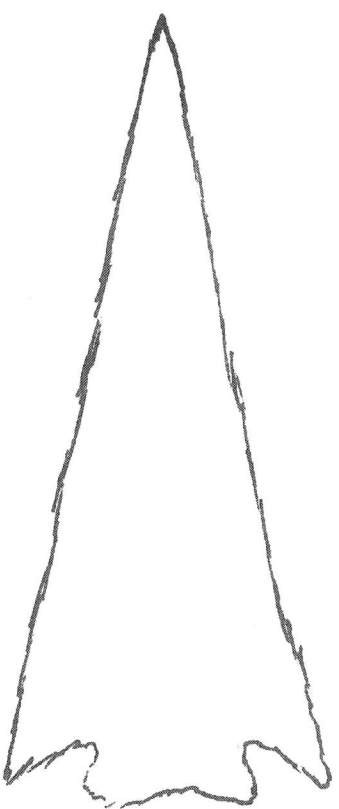

I was genuinely and truly impressed. By now, several of the others in the skinning shed had come to watch Henry's artwork. The entire assembly of onlookers was enthralled. Even the old master arrowhead collector, David Gonzales, was overwhelmed with Henry's find. When asked if he had such a specimen in his collection, David had to admit that although he might come close, he couldn't match the one Henry had recreated on paper.

"Holy Toledo, Henry." I could hardly find words to praise his great achievement. Looking closely now at his drawing, I just had to be sure that I understood the deal. The specimen in that drawing was virtually flawless.

"You mean to tell me, Mr. Dusek, that you actually found an arrowhead that looks exactly like that image you have created?" I waited for his confirmation. There was a long, long pause.

Henry finally, reluctantly admitted, "Well, not exactly." Grabbing up his pencil once again, he drew a horizontal line about a half-inch below the tip of the point. Pointing at the small end of his drawing now, Henry confessed.

"Actually," he disclosed, "I just found this part right here."

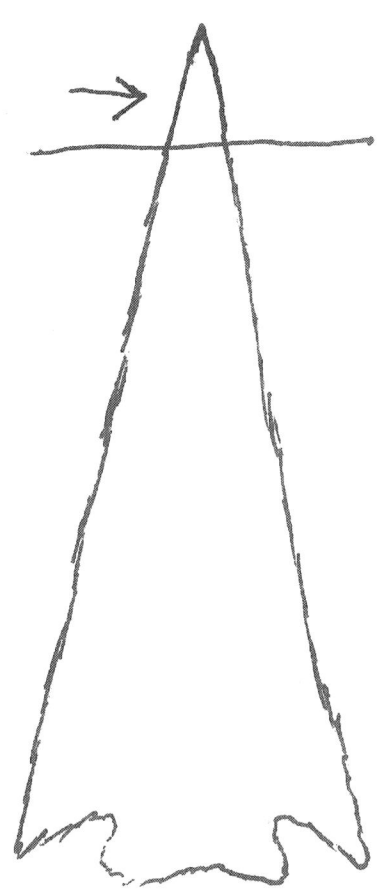

POETRY

Until I was about 7 years old, my parents lived in the 1900 Block of Concho Avenue which, in those late days of the 1940s, was right on the edge of San Angelo. I had a Shetland pony to prowl the vacant lots and mesquite flats to the west. That neighborhood today is right in the middle of town and is miles away from the city limits. As it is said: Time changes everything.

In those days of long ago, across the street from us lived a lady who was a sure-enough poet. In fact, a few years later Mildred Lindsay Raiborn was the Poet Laureate of Texas for a couple of years. In watching my antics on that little horse, Ms. Raiborn composed the following poem which my mother had framed beneath a photo of me and Lady, the pony.

Birth of a Cowboy

A Shetland cowboy rides over the land,
Frolicking, galloping into the wind,
Playing the reins in his new bridle hand
As laughter and hoof-beats musically blend.

Tales Galore: And a Whole Lot More

Gracefully swaying high in his saddle
As late he rode on his horse made of wood,
While roaming the house on his steed astraddle
And seeking mischief wherever he could.

My heart calls him back while I let him go
And fashion a smile as he waves good-bye.
The breezes whisper his far-off "Heigh-ho!"
Toy silhouette on a blue tinted sky.

And now the silence is loud in my ears . . .
A change has been marked by the passing years.
                    Mildred Lindsey Raiborn, c 1949

So being the subject of a genuine poem by an accredited poet, that might have been a catalyst of some kind. That photo and poem hung in Mom's house until the day she died. It was a family heirloom and that poem was something Mom cherished.

It would be a while before poetry was once again written about little old me. About 15 years, come to think of it.

Decades before cowboy poets such as Baxter Black and Waddie Mitchell came along to perform their clever and wonderful lyrics at the National Cowboy Poetry Gathering in Elko, Nevada, my old buddy, Tommy Nasworthy, with a stubby pencil and some notebook paper, sat down one time to create a jingle. He was the first cowboy I ever knew to pen a rhyme.

Tommy composed the ditty to make fun of my poor roping abilities which had been on full exhibit in his practice pen on his Menard ranch. His cadence and rhyming were far from perfect, but neither was my roping, so I guess we were even. As they say: "It's the thought that counts." Here's how Tommy's lines went:

A tall and dashing cowboy I once knew
While trying to tie a calf in ten-two
Did get in a jam like I never saw before
Or doubt whether I will ever once more.

He roped the calf and bailed off fast
Then stuck his head in the reins and hit on his ass.
He jumped up with the speed of a gazelle
Grabbed the calf by the leg then slipped and fell.

All at once he screamed out in loud pain
Then turned loose the calf right where he had lain
Then he cried and cussed and muttered "Oh, heck!"
For this little calf had pissed down his neck.
Tommy Nasworthy c 1961

Of course, upon receiving a missive of that order, a rebuttal was clearly in order. I composed a page-long poem making fun of one of Tommy's recent horseback hunting trips to Colorado. I suppose these events spawned my career as a poet.

During my calf roping days, when I traveled over long stretches of highways in the dark of the night, I needed something to keep me awake. The most effective tool for this purpose was an Echo harmonica. This particular brand made by Hohner has a double-set of reeds top and bottom (hence the "Echo" name) and produces a completely different sound than regular harmonicas played by my music buddies Bill Armstrong, Jr. and Max Hulse (who died a few years ago.) I was able to play the thing while driving my rig with one hand. After a few months of practice, I could play almost any tune I could whistle.

I am woefully incompetent when it comes to remembering important things. Names of grasses, shrubs, bushes and trees on the ranch bewilder me although I have been told their names countless times by range expert, Steve Nelle. Most all birds of a similar size look exactly alike to me and despite the fact that I have been instructed over and over by my buddy and bird expert, Ross Dawkins, I can't tell you one from the other.

I cannot remember the names of stars or of geological formations. I'm not too good with names of people. But by golly, I can remember the words to scores of songs. So playing that harmonica, I could sing along in my mind sounding exactly like whoever I wanted to sound like. If only I had been born with a voice like Tex Ritter. One of my favorite singers was Marty Robbins. I had an album of his classic cowboy songs and knew every one of them by heart.

To my thinking, one of his best songs was *"Strawberry Roan"*, the old cowboy classic that tells of the cocky young bronc rider who was hired to break the outlaw horse. It's a great tune with wonderful lyrics. In playing that melody on my harmonica while traveling to and from various ropings here and there, it dawned on me that few songs had ever been written about ropers. The only one of any note was the old verse about Buster Jiggs and Sandy Bob tying a knot in the Devil's tail after they had head-and-heeled him. Calf ropers, on the other hand, have been virtually ignored in American musicana. Bronc riders get all the attention.

So as I drove along the rodeo trail, I began to right that wrong. Trouble was, I might be able to come up with some words, but I needed a tune. Heck fire – why not use the old Strawberry Roan tune and theme? Virtual plagiarism is the easiest alternative for us no-talent types, especially when a tune is in the public domain and there is no chance of a lawsuit. So using that famous old melody and borrowing many of the same words along the way, here is a calf roper's version of Strawberry Roan. I also stole many of Hal Churchill's descriptive words about the sport of calf roping.

*I was hanging around town, just spending my time
With no entry fees cause I ain't won a dime.
A feller steps up and he says "I suppose
You're a calf roper from the looks of your clothes."*

*"You're damn right I am, and I'm damn good I boast.
Do you happen to have any bad ones to rope?"
He says he's got some that ain't been marked yet,
And if I tie 'em down, then a hundred I'll get.*

*He says "Get your saddle and bring all your ropes."
I follows him to his ranch in a high lope.
I stays until morning and with the first light
I steps out to see if his dogies can fight.*

*Down in the roping pen standing alone
Are some black Brangus heifers with a little fine bone.
But they're fat and they're slick, weighing way over three
They trots up and down just a-glaring at me.*

*I saddles old Bay and I gets out my rope.
If I don't tie 'em down, I'm gonna be broke.
They load up the chute as I ride in the box.
I tightens my cinch to the very last notch.*

*I gets back in the corner to get me a start
They opens the gate and she comes with a snort.
I sees 'bout her shoulder then comes in a run
But she's gone from there like a shot from a gun.*

*She ducks first to the left and then to the right.
But old Bay ain't fooled, he's a-comin' up tight.
I kicks him up close, 'cause she ain't no pup,
And I know I want to be there when she gets up.*

Well I cranks-up and throws and throat-latches that sow.
Old Bay starts to stop and he really knows how.
He sits on his tail and up boils the dirt.
He clinches his teeth, and he waits for that jerk.

I gets off the right to start me a run
That heifer's legs pointed right up to the sun.
The first thing that hits is the back of her head.
With a fall like that, she should'a been dead.

But I'm two steps away when she comes off the ground.
She lowers her head, and then runs me down.
She steps in my pocket and tears off my shirt
And leaves me with nothing but a mouthful of dirt.

I grabs her front leg and she starts to fall down
But kicks hard at my crotch before hitting the ground.
I strings her front leg, she sticks her toe in my eye.
I have to slow down and tie one leg at a time.

There's forty more calves – it gets nothing but worse.
When the long day is over, I'm needing a hearse.
I collects me my money, but I'll be mighty low
If I draw one like them at the old rodeo.
Skipper Duncan c 1969

So after this magnificent effort, I composed no poetry or songs for several years. There were plenty of other activities to occupy my time, and besides, I knew few wealthy poets. None, as a matter of fact. I just continued to rehearse the song in my head while playing that harmonica on long trips.

Several years went by. All of a sudden, seemed like, major birthdays began to come upon friends who were growing older. When my good quail hunting buddy, Dr. Bob Hamblen turned 40, I had no idea what kind of present might work for him. He had every toy imaginable. So just for the heck of it, I wrote him a poem. And he loved it. Even had the thing framed for his wall. Unlike me who had been the subject and beneficiary of a couple of poems, Bob declared my poem was the first he had received.

So when Bob turned 50, and then 60 a decade later, I composed more verses for his amusement. He added them to his collection. A few years later, Bob's wife, Cybee, invited Jeri and me to his birthday party when he turned 66. As we arrived at the party, Cybee said I was to read the poem I had written for Bob. What poem? I didn't know they expected one. But I did have a track record to uphold so I quickly composed the following jingle:

You only get a card this year
A verse you do not win.

I only write a birthday poem
If you can divide your age by ten.

But that first poem for Bob Hamblen started the trend. When friends would hit big birthdays or when they would retire, I'd whip out my yellow pad and try to put together a few lines poking fun at their traits as I saw them.

Back in the mid-1960s, I got to know a local highway patrolman, Brantley Foster. We were big buddies at the time, although it was a bit disconcerting to see his black and white patrol car on my ranch road when he stopped by to visit. I even accompanied him one night on his rounds and gained a new appreciation for that dangerous work done by law officers when they walk up to a car they have stopped. No telling what awaits them sitting behind that steering wheel. Heretofore, highway cops had been my enemy. Not anymore.

Brantley was finally transferred away and I saw no more of him until several years later when he showed up unannounced at the ranch. He was still with the Texas Department of Public Safety, but now he was working on drug details as an undercover officer. I hardly recognized him with his long pony tail and flowery shirt. Next I heard, he had become a full-fledged Texas Ranger, that being one of the most storied law enforcement agencies in the nation. And then, as the years flew by, I got an invitation to his retirement party. I had learned that Brantley now lived in Mt. Pleasant and owned cutting horses. Unfortunately, I was unable to attend the function, but I sent the following poem which was said to be a hit at the gathering.

The Retirement of
Texas Ranger Sergeant Brantley Foster
1965 – 1993

A ranger retires after twenty-eight years
Although he's still working good.
Somehow he's survived a dangerous job
Catching robbers and killers and hoods.

A '65 model isn't really used up
Though that model was a memorable date.
But a '65 model with only twenty-eight years
Gets no commemorative plates.

How do we turn out to pasture a man
Who still looks great when he smiles?
Like an old black-and-white from the year '65,
It isn't the age, it's the miles.

Unlike some horse who's won every race,
Genetically Brantley's a dud.

Now in retirement, it's a sure bet
He's not being put out to stud.
Skipper Duncan, 1993

So by now, writing poems for friend's big events became a duty and obligation. As my good buddy, Vic Choate, who had been turning perfectly gray-headed for the past 15 years, came upon his 40th birthday, my poem to him ended with these two verses:

None can explain it, though we've all talked about
If Vic is forty today,
Can he keep up the pace he has set for himself
As he breaks into deep middle age?

As I ponder this question, I have a new thought:
Vic's already gray ear-to-ear
Vic will do OK as a 40-year-old.
He's looked like he's 40 for years.

Well now, come to find out, Vic Choate is one heck of a poet, too. Unknown to me, Vic had been writing similar poems for friends' special events for quite some time. Not only that, Vic writes a poem each year for a celebration hosted by the entire Choate family on Thanksgiving morning. Yes, you noticed. Thanksgiving morning is when that special event occurs. West Texans never forego an opportunity to party and I guess that was the only time not yet on anyone's calendar. Anyway,

VIC CHOATE

Vic's annual rhyme at that unique event is always the climax of the morning.

Now when it comes to cowboy poets, Vic Choate is the real deal. Following in the footsteps of his dad, Wade Choate, Vic is an order buyer and cow trader. He spends more time a-horseback than most of the ranchers I know. And the Choate's have a pen full of good horses. But one of them came untrained one time when Vic was 49 years old. So naturally, for his 50th birthday hosted by his wife Cathy, I just had to compose a few words:

Vic Makes It to Fifty, Barely

Cowboys are tough, and their edges are rough
Those bovines demand it of them.
It's famine, not feast, for the biggest and least.
Vic's a cowboy – a rough, un-cut gem.

The Choate's horses aren't phony, but a good set of ponies.
They're rode hard and put up all wet.
But with so many good ones, Vic chose a plumb dumb one
Not suspecting the ride he would get.

Vic was surprised, when his horse from him shied
And ran away down through the trees.
Vic's face sure was smashed, in that 100-yard dash
So we all prayed to God on our knees —-

To keep him alive and again let him thrive
And to guide those who labored for hours
To patch up his wounds, so again just real soon
Old Vic could stand tall like a tower.

Though long did he suffer, he's now fully recovered –
But Cathy thinks they got a "rookin".
To remake Vic's face and put it all back in place –
For the fee, they should-a made Vic better looking.

At the same they could've, indeed they sure should've
During surgery as Vic lay on their bed,
With a snip and a tuck and a bit of good luck
Implanted a cell phone in his head.

Skipper Duncan, 2001

Thank You, Jesus. Vic did, indeed, fully recover from that bad wreck. It wasn't long until he was back to riding horses, working cattle and writing his good poems, too. He is kind enough to send most of them on to me whether I know the intended recipient or not.

Vic's poems are mighty clever, but they do sting a bit if you are the target. Here's one by the "Bard of Mt. Nebo." (Mt. Nebo is the prominent butte north of San Angelo near the Choate's extensive cattle pens and headquarters.)

Happy Birthday Skipper dear
We're glad at 70 you're still here.
If we make jest please do not fear.
We're pretty sure you cannot hear.

You cannot see.
You cannot pee.
And sex - - -is just a memory.
A distant one at seventy.

These golden years are maybe brass.
Now you are in a different class.

Tales Galore: And a Whole Lot More

*We're sure you'd like to take a pass
Or maybe—-simply pass some gas.*

*But, hey, you ain't dead yet
Worry not. Dare not fret.
For ne'er a stranger you've ever met
And that's a pretty damn good bet.*

*You can try
To philosophy
But it's pie in the sky
When your well goes dry.*

*There is one thing we should discuss
We all would like to make a fuss.
I think I speak for all of us.
To us—you've been a great big plus.*

*You've organized the "gathering"
You're known around here as the hunting king.
You can pick a little and sorta sing
We think you can do anything.*

*You can rope a steer.
You can shoot a deer.
And drinking beer –
You have no peer.*

*You can turn a rhyme
To have a good time
And your hospitality's sublime.*

*I know this sounds like a lotta wind
But the truth, you know, we would not bend*

From top to top and end to end
To all of us you're a damn good friend.
                              Vic Choate, August 28, 2011

Evidently, not everyone appreciates good poetry. The quadrennial election of a president was under way, and I felt duty bound to make a donation to my candidate's party. Big mistake. By the time it was all over, I had accumulated a box full of letters from them now since they had the address of someone gullible enough to send money to their cause.

To properly address the issue at a national level, I submitted the following poem to the Reader's Digest. I thought for sure I would receive the promised $300 for contributions to their rag. They did not. But they should have.

I think it's smart to do my part
To keep up with the news,
And contribute money to worthy groups
Which best reflect my views.

Now I'm confused how my funds are used
And I don't think it's funny.
My donation goes for more mail-outs
To dun ME for more money.
                              Skipper Duncan, 2000

So why all the poems for birthdays, retirements and special occasions?

As you might imagine, there is a powerful reason. Indeed, I have discussed the subject with my amigo and fellow poet, Vic Choate. We are both of like minds on the subject. Come to find out, we work in a similar fashion on a project. Like me, Vic composes poetry while driving. Almost always, the final verse will be written first. Both of us scribble test lines on a pad, working out the jingle by trial and error.

So what's the answer to the question above? The query wasn't "how," but "why?"

The answer is abundantly apparent and, of course, I composed a short verse to explain it. In the interest of full disclosure, I have used the following stanza as a postscript on several poems written for friends to explain my motives:

To rhyme a few lines takes plenty of time,
But it's done so a spirit will lift.

The reason is clear, the solution so near –
Cowboy poets are too cheap to buy gifts.

Pranksters

If every human on the planet was as serious as NFL coaches on Sunday afternoons during the fall, we'd all miss out on lots of fun. It has been my good fortune to be around some jim-dandy prank-players. Their shenanigans are the spice of life.

Years ago during the early days of my outfitting business, a civil engineer from New York City hunted with us. He was a most interesting fellow and told one hell of a tale. Sitting around the old fire pit one night, he remembered his earlier work in helping build a tunnel below the Hudson River. It was a huge undertaking to be sure. As the story went, two tunnels were begun at each end of the project. The two shafts under construction were to meet somewhere in the middle. Apparently, that's the way such construction jobs are done.

Trouble was, the head superintendent of the task was a real jerk. Month after month, he became increasingly unbearable. Everyone on the mission despised him. So the engineers on the project concocted a scheme to teach the top dog a lesson. As each day's removal of dirt was recorded, the conspirators would prepare their reports to show that more dirt was being removed than was actually the case. They fudged the numbers somehow.

The head man was measuring the progress on each end of the tunnel by calculating the volume of dirt removed. He had determined the exact day when the two tunnels should meet. But when the day arrived that the two should be joined, it didn't happen. As you might imagine, he was horrified. He slaved over all the months of data fearing that somehow, some way, his calculations were in error.

Of course, everything was right on schedule and the two tunnels were aimed right at each other. That misinformation gave the chief one heck of a headache.

No one I know has been guilty of pulling off a trick of this magnitude. But there have been a-plenty that were entertaining to say the least. Two of my good friends, Tommy Buckner and Bob Hamblen, were/are unrepentant prank-players. Tragically, Tommy died in an airplane crash a number of years ago. Dr. Bob Hamblen has now mostly retired both from his practice of anesthesiology and from trick-playing. Detailing the stunts these two pulled off during the height of their respective careers would fill a large file cabinet.

Tommy Buckner

Tommy Buckner and I became friends during my final year at Texas Tech. After college, we became super-amigos and stayed in close touch. Tommy went on to earn a master's degree and taught at South Plains

Tommy Buckner.jpg

College in Levelland (just west of Lubbock) for a couple of years. Then, as I recall, he sold cars in Lamesa for a year or so. Next, he moved to the northern panhandle to look after wheat pasture cattle in an effort to get involved in the feedlot business. It worked. Wasn't long until he was named manager of the Nor-Tex cattle feeders at Dalhart.

Even back in our college days, Tommy was a dedicated horse trader. Having a father who made his living selling used cars and horses, Tommy had been born into the business. Wheeling and dealing was in his DNA. Cattle deals are a daily occurrence around a feedlot and Tommy was in his element. He was by then an old hand at buying and selling. Moreover, he was an extrovert's extrovert. He never met a stranger and I'll bet few people who crossed his path ever forgot him. To say that Tommy was entertaining is a giant understatement. Things were never dull in his presence.

His best horse-trading conspirator back at college had been Louis Marshall, cut out of the same bolt of cloth as was Tommy. They kept a perpetual ad running in the Lubbock Avalanche-Journal offering horses for sale. No matter the kind of horse you might be looking for – they had it. Or would describe it as such to your satisfaction.

College classmate horseshoers Clayton Friend and Burney (Wichita) Chapman were victims of one of their pranks. An ad appeared in the Lubbock paper offering registered quarter horse fillies for the ridiculously low price of $50 each. The ad listed Clayton's phone number. He must have fielded scores of calls before he was finally able to get the ad cancelled. Clayton had no doubt about the source of this grief.

Not to be outdone, Clayton ran his own classified ad a few days later offering "Percheron Guineas" for sale , specifically 3 "ferdis" and 4 "condras". This gibberish was followed with Louis Marshall's phone number with the admonition to call before 6 a.m. or after 10 p.m.

Louis and Tommy were quite a pair. Louis could beat any living human playing tennis or shooting pool. With Tommy handling all the betting on either contest, they easily financed their horse trading activities. Tommy's role, of course, was to set the trap for the sting by misrepresenting Louis' incredible skills. When he set his mind to it, Tommy could charm the birds out of the trees.

As time went on and as our friendship developed, Tommy never grew tired of embarrassing me at any opportunity. I was always gullible for any of his mischiefs. For example, if I happened to be stopped at a red light in downtown San Angelo with Tommy in the passenger seat, he would reach across the cab of my truck to sound the horn if a nice-looking girl happened to walk in front of us. Of course, the girl would turn and give ME the "go-to-hell" look instead of directing it toward the guilty party, Tommy. I must be a slow learner. He succeeded in shaming me numerous times to my everlasting embarrassment. Time after time he could get his hand on that horn before I could stop him.

His most outrageous stunt was pulled during a most unlikely time. It was on the day of his father's funeral. I had gone up to Big Spring to be with him all day to help in whatever capacity might be needed. Their home was on East 4th Street, the main highway through the city, and the vacant lot next door was crowded with relatives' vehicles. There were scores of people dropping by all day long. Tommy was busy greeting one and all, helping his mother cope with the loss of her husband of many years.

Finally Tommy needed a break from the crush of people. He quietly told me he wanted to go get some cigars which we both smoked on an irregular basis. We hopped in my pickup with him directing our journey to an old-fashioned newsstand and tobacco shop in downtown Big Spring near the old Settles Hotel. You never see such businesses anymore.

As we entered the establishment, a couple of "blue-haired little old ladies" were in deep conversation with the proprietor, who was standing behind the counter and who, herself, could be described with the exact same words. They might as well have been triplets – all nice, proper gentlewomen. The two elderly visitors stood right outside the huge glass display counter which held the impressive array of cigar boxes and tins of pipe tobacco. The third lady was clearly in charge of the business. Their quiet conversation probably dealt with the latest covered dish meal at their church.

Tommy had mentioned his goal of buying cigars. I took him at his word. We had come to purchase tobacco, and I was trying to make my selection. The nearby biddies chattered away. Tommy had disappeared somewhere and ignored the tobacco.

I was within arms-length of the two visitors. I made my wishes known to the shop owner who momentarily interrupted her conversation to retrieve my purchase from the display case.

Just at that very moment, Tommy showed up from behind us. He was hoisting one of those "XXX Rated" magazines he had found in the rear of the store. Using both hands to hold the thing open to the huge centerfold photo, he dominated the area with his find. The image left nothing to the imagination. He waved it right in my face. I wanted to melt into the floor. He assumed a demeanor of shock and announced forcefully:

"SKIPPER. YOU WON'T BELIEVE WHAT KINDS OF PHOTOS THEY ARE PUTTING IN MAGAZINES THESE DAYS. HAVE YOU EVER SEEN ANYTHING LIKE THIS BEFORE?"

The three ladies couldn't help but get an eyeful. After one brief glance, I turned in horror to face the others in the audience.

Of course, all three proper women eyed me with something between disgust and contempt. They dismissed Tommy. He was the guilty party, but I was charged with the crime. How the hell he pulled off that stunt, I'll never know. The three offended women glared at me as if that outrageous photo was somehow my fault. All I wanted at that point was "out of there" and to heck with any cigars.

Not many people were ever able to pull a fast one on Tommy Buckner. One of the very few was another feedlot manager, Bill Thorne, Tommy's good friend and neighbor. Back in the days when the "Urban Cowboy" fad had invaded the nation, Bill Thorne procured one of those ridiculous huge feathers that adorned the front of a cowboy hat. In league with Tommy's bank, Bill had the outlandish thing gift wrapped. He talked Tommy's banker into delivering the box to Tommy as the bank's annual Christmas present to their good customers. Tommy, expecting the bank's traditional ham, told Bill Thorne that he would never wear the offensive feather on anything, much less his cowboy hat. Bill kept the sting going by warning Tommy that all the bank people would be highly offended if they didn't see Tommy using their gift. Heck, they might even refuse to handle his banking business in the future.

BILL THORNE

On another occasion, the assistant manager at Bill's feedlot, Les Howard, was trading mules. In passing by one day, Tommy spotted some miniature donkeys in the mule pens and made a disparaging comment about the utter uselessness of such animals. Overhearing Tommy's criticism, Bill Thorne lost no time in buying a couple of the little donkeys knowing that they could, in fact, be put to good use. He just had a brainstorm.

Tommy's daughter, Bonnie, had a birthday coming up. She was going to be 8 or 9 and was the apple of her Daddy's eye. Thorne was ready for this event. On the big day, he produced a huge sign saying "Happy Birthday, Bonnie. Love, Dad." He put the little jackasses in Tommy's dog pen where they would be the first thing Bonnie saw after school. Bonnie was so effusive with her thanks to her dad that he was obliged to keep the worthless critters for several weeks. Bonnie named them "Bo" and "Peep." With Bonnie, the miniature burros were as gentle as could be. But with either Tommy or any of the cowboys in his employ, the little critters would buck and pitch like NFR champions, which further infuriated Tommy. The old horse trader/bronc peeler had met his match.

Because I was the perpetual butt of all Tommy's pranks, I always cheered when Bill Thorne would win a round every now and then with the master trickster. Despite all Tommy's successes in getting my goat, I rarely ever scored any points in a matchup with him. In restaurants after meals when the bills came, Tommy would invariably insist that we "split it right down the middle – 60/40."

Tommy Buckner's motto was simple: *"Act like you know what you are doing, then go ahead and do it."* He once succeeded in driving a friend's motor home all over the floor of the Astrodome in Houston. No one had the presence of mind to stop him and inquire if he had a right to be there.

Once at a cattlemen's convention in Dallas, according to Bill Thorne, Tommy succeeded in getting his entire party, including his in-laws, front-row seats to hear George H.W. Bush only because Tommy had the audacity to enter the hall early through the kitchen despite the abundant presence of Secret Service throughout the hotel.

He was fearless in such matters and never worried about hearing the word "NO." Being the lifelong horse trader that he was, he would interpret that admonition as simply being a point at which to start a negotiation. By the end of the deal, Tommy would have exactly what he wanted while his adversary would have morphed into full support of his plan.

Not all of Tommy's schemes were mischievous. Every now and then, he would concoct a program to correct a miscarriage of justice. Several pen riders were employed at that feedlot he managed. It was the duty of these sho'nuff cowboys to prowl a-horseback through all the cattle pens each day checking for sick or distressed cattle. About mid-morning, they would gather at the saddle room back at the horse pens for coffee, conversation and current news. Another feedlot employee, Dexter, would be there, too. Dexter was no part of a cowboy – he cleaned the numerous water troughs around the huge feedlot and made minor repairs where needed. The aloof cowboys considered Dexter to be their inferior and never included him in their elite group. Dexter would sit all alone on the far side of the barn drinking his coffee.

Periodically, Tommy would stop by the room to touch base with all the hands. He was interested in the condition of the cattle and received the cowboy's verbal reports of what they were finding. It wasn't long until Tommy noticed that Dexter was habitually ignored. So on future visits, Tommy would take his cup of coffee to the far end of the barn and spend his time exclusively with Dexter. After a time or two of hanging out only with Dexter, the cowboys began to drift to Dexter's end of the barn to participate in conversation with their boss, Tommy.

When Tommy noticed that all the cowboys were within earshot, he began to praise Dexter's work, especially the critical task of keeping clean water for the cattle. Just in passing, Tommy happened to note that if it wasn't for that wholesome water, the cowboys would be working twice as hard doctoring sick cattle. He went on and on with his commendation of Dexter's contribution to the entire program at the feedlot. As you might imagine, from then on, the cowboys developed a particular fondness for Dexter and considered him in a brand new light. Finally, he was accepted as a full-fledged member of their team.

Tommy Buckner was a good, good friend, and I learned one heck of a lot from him about cattle, horses and trading. Being one of the most energetic people I've ever known, he crammed an 80-year life into the 50-some he was given. There were tears a-plenty among all us pallbearers at his funeral, but they were tears of laughter as we rode in the limousine to the cemetery. Everyone had his own memory of some outrageous prank Tommy had pulled. It was a fitting way to handle the collective grief we all shared.

Sadly, Tommy Buckner won't be honking at pretty girls from my truck anymore.

Tales Galore: And a Whole Lot More

Bob Hamblen

After playing only one minor trick on Bob Hamblen and after suffering his dastardly reprisal (paybacks are hell), I petitioned for a peace treaty. And so it came to pass. The sordid details of that long-ago event are chronicled in my earlier book, *Characters and Critters*. The two of us made amends and retired from trick-playing on each other. Future targets, especially for him, were fair game.

Bob Hamblen took the game of pranks to majestic levels. He chose his victims wisely over the years. Proof of this fact is that no one ever tried to kill him for revenge. But if they had, no jury, after examining the evidence, would have voted for conviction of the murderer. Bob was an unrepentant guilty conspirator.

Who the heck is Bob Hamblen? Born in the 1930s, he grew up in the Dallas area, the second son of an autocratic but loving father. His uncle, Stuart Hamblen, was a famous personality and songwriter (*"It Is No Secret What God Can Do"; "This Ole House"*). Early on, Bob was competitive as all get-out, probably because he was the smallest brother. Being short in stature, he learned he could contend with others his size in a boxing ring. So he became a Golden Gloves boxer and learned to fight.

In college, he first earned a degree in geology of all things. But his interests turned to medicine, and he chose that as his profession. Early on, he focused on becoming a pediatrician and gained those credentials. Sometime along about then, he decided to switch horses in the middle of the stream and became an anesthesiologist. So finally, that was his new career. Admittedly dyslectic, Bob credits his careful listening to his success in college. Although he read slowly and kept poor notes, none of those handicaps held him back. He had (and still has) an incredible drive toward success. Even with his challenges in reading, he inhales books and is one of the best-read people I know.

Bob moved to San Angelo in the early 1970s with his wife Cybee (pronounced See Bee) and his three kids, Bettye, Andy and Allen. Our involvement in the First Presbyterian Church first brought us together. Bob, being addicted to guns and hunting, probably saw me as being someone he should get to know better since I owned a ranch loaded with game. It wasn't long until we teamed up to hunt quail. Back during those mystical days, I had blues and bob whites coming out of my ears. We both quickly became addicted to the new sport of hunting birds with dogs. It wasn't long until we became great, great friends – and still are some 40 years later.

Dr. Bob Hamblen

Bob was easy to like. He continually poked fun at himself, especially his height. To be sure, he ain't very tall, but truthfully, I never really noticed his perceived handicap. Bob regularly referred to himself as "Tall, Dark, and Handsome." He even had those words stenciled in large, colorful letters on the back of the scrub jacket he always wore in the operating room. My sainted Mother, when she got to know Bob better and better as he patiently helped her through several medical calamities, avowed that Bob was "the tallest person she ever knew."

Another mighty assertion from Bob goes like this: "My heart is pure. And I have the strength of ten."

To which Cybee once famously replied: "Yes, and the B.S. of twenty."

Being an unrepentant extrovert, Bob was a hit with most all the medical professionals in the hospital. Until it became politically incorrect to do so, Bob would hug every female he encountered – patient, nurse, friend, foe. He was especially popular with his wide circle of friends. If surgery was prescribed for any of them, they would insist that Dr. Bob do the anesthesia. No doctor I ever knew had a better "bedside manner" than Dr. Bob. He set everyone's mind at ease about their upcoming surgical events. He knew his stuff and could explain complicated medical jargon so that everyone – patient, family and loved ones – would fully understand what to expect. And he treated all the same – rich or poor, famous or unknown, old or young, lovable or unlovable.

When interviewing a patient prior to entering the operating room, Dr. Bob would explain that the anesthesia is probably the most life-threatening part of the procedure. He likened it to driving a car down a wet highway. But he would offer a guarantee. "I get extra help for you, your surgeon, the OR nurses, the OR techs and myself from The Big Boss upstairs."

But even being the cherished physician he was, there was this penchant for pranks lurking in his chemical makeup. Taking a detached view of this diabolical trait he possessed, one would have to conclude that his targets were mainly those he held in high esteem. He really, really enjoyed "getting their goat." Many are the times during a quail hunt when he would recount his latest sting. All the surgeons with whom he worked were continually vulnerable.

One unfortunate surgeon, Dr. Larry Bragg, suffered a string of miseries at Bob's hand. The locker room where the surgical team changed into their "scrubs" provided Bob with an opportunity to steal Dr. Bragg's car keys. He quickly dashed to Dix Key Shop, only a few blocks away, and had duplicates made before returning the purloined keys to their original location without detection. Now he was prepared for his mischief.

Between cases, and in checking the schedule of his prey in order to remain undetected, Bob would slip out of the hospital to relocate Bragg's car to a different location in the doctor's parking lot. Of course, the first time this happened, the bewildered surgeon thought his car had been stolen and reported it as such.

Over the course of the next several weeks (months?), Larry Bragg, upon leaving the hospital for the day, faced the challenge of locating his car. Sometimes it would finally be found in the visitor's parking lot across the street.

The continuing vehicle disappearance probably didn't have anything to do with his decision, but some time later, Dr. Bragg relocated himself and his practice to another Texas hospital in Stephenville, 150 miles to the east. As luck would have it, Bob just happened to be good buddies with another anesthesiologist in that new venue. He lost no time in shipping the keys to his comrade to continue the misery for the poor Dr. Bragg . If the unfortunate surgeon had ever suspected Bob Hamblen back in San Angelo, how could he be guilty now? They were presently miles apart.

Without a doubt, the most long suffering target for Bob's mischief was Sonny Cleere.

Sonny is a partner in one of San Angelo's premier insurance agencies. At first glance, you would never pick Sonny to be vulnerable to any of Hamblen's schemes. They are about the same age. Both are highly motivated and energetic. Both are successful in their chosen careers. Both are early-risers which will become important to the story as it unfolds.

But that's where their similarities end.

Sonny is a big guy. In fact, he played college football as a guard and linebacker and ran track as a sprinter. His distinctive manner of speech features a deep, resonate voice with a perfect cadence and elocution. So equipped, he often provides announcing services for many civic functions and athletic contests.

On the surface at least, Sonny seems to be extremely formal without an ounce of horseplay in his demeanor. Almost always, he is impeccably groomed and could pass himself off as a diplomat working at the highest levels in government. He admits to being exceedingly disciplined and a creature of habit. His daily routine varies not in minutes but in seconds.

SONNY CLEERE

Bob Hamblen and Sonny Cleere became acquaintances when they began to work out at the Shannon Hospital's exercise facility. If you can believe it, the brutal hour of their workout began at 5 a.m. Bob, of course, had to be at the nearby hospital to make his rounds before the surgery activities began at 7 or so. Super-early exercise programs were his only alternative. At the facility, almost always, it would be only Bob and Sonny Cleere on site at that early hour.

After several weeks, Bob began to notice that the regimented Sonny always parked his car in the exact same spot every morning. With more than 200 available places to choose from, the disciplined Sonny would time his arrival to be at the door when it opened at 5 a.m. and, no doubt, he knew just how many seconds it would take to make the walk from that special parking place to the front door. This structured routine was perfect for the devious Bob Hamblen. He carefully made his plans.

To set things in motion, one fine morning Bob arrived at the parking lot at 4:45 and encroached on Sonny's parking spot. When Sonny arrived, of course he had no choice but to park his car elsewhere. But he did not like this interruption to his schedule. He simply could not abide such an inconvenience. So the next morning, Sonny showed up at 4:30 to claim his traditional place on the vast lot. Characteristically, neither man mentioned the unfolding drama during their times in the gym. Next time, Bob arrived at 4:15. Later on, Sonny, not to be outdone, arrived at 4 a.m.

Back and forth it went until both men were arriving at the parking lot at 3 a.m. or so. Finally, the subject was discussed and a truce was called. Sonny, being a magnanimous and forgiving person, held no grudges over the deal, but now, Bob had learned he had a new victim for his pranks. They became close friends and even went on a dove hunting trip to Mexico with a group of San Angelo pals.

It was on that fateful trip that Bob learned another of Sonny's traits. Way down in South Texas and over in old Mexico, blue indigo snakes can be found. They can grow to impressive lengths and appear quite fearsome although they are not venomous. Bob Hamblen has no fear of any kind of snake. During the hunt, he happened to catch one of the indigo reptiles and brought it back to the group of hunters. Quickly Bob learned that Sonny has an inborn, visceral hatred of snakes – any kind, any species, any length, poisonous or not. To Sonny, a snake is a snake, and he wants nothing to do with them. If only Bob Hamblen had not learned this, Sonny's future would have been more tolerable. But the clever doctor did take note of the insurance man's fears. It was a momentous event.

Once back home and once back to their early morning exercise programs at the health facility, Bob began to employ the use of snakes to torment his victim. Bob had killed a rattlesnake somewhere on his farm and brought the dead serpent to the gym. He put the carcass in the corner of the shower where Sonny would freshen up after his workout. Just imagine the terror that struck Sonny when he finally spotted the reptile in his shower facility. A wet dead snake looks amazingly alive. Without a stitch of clothes on our bodies or shoes on our feet, any of us would be especially mortified with a close encounter of that kind. Sonny tore the door off the room in making his exit.

Sonny never varied his workout routine, so Bob knew within seconds of when Sonny would be on a mat doing his half-sit-ups or "crunches." Some days later, Bob crept up to the overhead balcony above the gym floor. Using a length of monofilament, Bob lowered a dead snake to be right in Sonny's face about halfway through his program. Poor Sonny exploded off the floor and raced away, his heart rate going off the charts, no doubt.

That clear fishing line was employed for yet another snake deal. Bob used it to tie one more dead snake to Sonny's gym bag. As Sonny grabbed his gear to depart one morning, the unnoticed but securely attached snake followed Sonny. When someone hollered "snake" and Sonny looked back, he took off like a rocket. But to his dismay, the snake followed his flight across the room. No matter his speed, that snake maintained its same distance behind. Sonny could not out-run the following menace. All he had to do was to drop his bag, but who could think of such a thing at a time like that?

Bob loved to hear Sonny's deep, resonate voice rise to a soprano's pitch after every encounter with serpents: *"Good Gawd-Aw-Mighty,"* he would screech.

When Bob Hamblen announced his retirement, Cybee and the family hosted a giant party. The invitation list included Bob's co-workers, associated doctors and surgeons, and his impressive collection of amigos of all kinds. After the scrumptious meal, attendees were invited to share "Bob Hamblen" stories. They came in abundance. Many, many people told delightful tales about the star of the show.

My contribution, of course, was yet one more poem for Bob. With this final effort, no doubt he would be fully equipped to cover the bottom of his bird cage.

Bob Hamblen's Retirement
January 29, 2011

You say Hamblen is quitten? You've got to be shitten.
This day must be only a dream.

He's been here forever. So how can he sever
His ties to the surgery team?

His bright disposition and long standing mission?
Bring cheer to all every day.

But there ain't no immunity in the medical community
To Hamblen and the pranks he will play.

Now about this retirement -

You know that he's earned it and the candle, he's burned it
At both ends for a mighty long time.

So toast him and roast him, now that he's coasting
To retirement on this miserable rhyme.

With Hamblen retired, no gas-passer hired
Could ever match what ole Hamblen has done.

So with Hamblen now gone, we'll sing this sad song -
SURGERY WILL NO LONGER BE FUN.

The highlight of the event was the presentation by Sonny Cleere. On that night of Bob's retirement and a virtual "roast" of his career, Sonny's remarks were unforgettable.

Remember it was said earlier that Sonny is an impressive public speaker. Few people could do a better job. In gracious good humor, Sonny detailed prank after prank he had endured at the hands of Bob Hamblen. Sonny's deadpan delivery of his outrageous sufferings brought the house down. With each new story he told, waves of laughter rose from the room. Of course, the snake stories were the hit of the talk, and by the time Sonny got to the last reptile yarn, we all had tears in our eyes.

Sonny brought his remarks to an end in a most memorable way. His summation went something like this:

So in conclusion, I want to tell you about the time that Bob Hamblen, himself, had to go see a doctor.

On the day of his appointment, with the doctor seated behind his desk, Bob walked into his office. Right away, the doctor noticed something very, very unusual.

Sitting there on the top of Bob's forehead was a large, green frog. The creature was impossible to ignore. Needless to say, the doctor was startled. He could not recall ever seeing such a sight, especially on a patient there in his office. This was a first.

Bob Hamblen remained mute, standing there in front of the doctor's desk.

Finally, the physician had the presence of mind to say something. He began simply.

"May I help you?"

And then THE FROG SAID: "I'm here to see if you can get this wart off of my ass."

THANKS

Finding a good editor for your writing is not an easy task.

For one thing, experienced editors have plenty of material to review in their regular jobs. Understandably, they are reluctant to take on additional work – especially the efforts of a non-professional. It's kind of like asking your local high school football coach to work with your son's sixth grade team during his spare time.

But a good editor is invaluable. Just go write something and polish those words to the best of your abilities. When you think you have it perfect, let an old-pro editor look it over to suggest a few changes here and there. You won't believe the improvement.

In my quest to find a good editor, my buddy Perry Flippin, the editor emeritus of our local San Angelo Standard Times, suggested Roy Ivey. Not only does Roy have a wealth of experience as a wordsmith, his background is pure-dee West Texas. He had no trouble in deciphering some of my mysterious rural tales. Getting Roy on the project was a stroke of luck. Beyond just being good at his craft, he was punctual, too. I didn't have to wait and wait to finally see his corrections.

Handling word documents on modern computers is just the cat's meow. You email your prose to your editor. With a few clicks of his mouse, he taps into an editing feature. If he finds a word that needs to be deleted, the magical computer will leave the old word in place with a horizontal line to strike it out. If a new word (or punctuation mark) needs to be added, that new addition will be in a bright color and easily found. So your editor makes his modifications along the way and can even add comments to explain his reasoning. When you get the corrected document back, you can readily see every change made.

Then, it was my choice to either accept or reject each change. I'm here to tell you Roy Ivey batted a thousand. I accepted every last suggested change because he nailed it. Thanks, Roy. I'm offering the traditional West Texas compliment here: "You done good."

Editors study the content. But to get a manuscript free of glitches, you also need a sharp-eyed proof-reader. Jackie Thompson did one heck of a job finding all manner of hiccups that both Roy and I had missed despite our numerous reviews of the prose. Yes, she is a retired teacher of English, but she hasn't lost her skill with that red pen to circle mistakes here and there on the double-spaced manuscript I had provided.

And once again, I called on my old buddy, Max Sanders, to review my work before shipping it to the printer. In a former life, Max was a research scientist who submitted numerous technical papers having to do with his studies of exercise and heart disease. You talk about someone being picky about writing the English language! Max, who also happened to be a Marine Corp drill instructor for a time, is a taskmaster if ever there was one. He'd rather find a split infinitive in my prose than a good arrowhead at my ranch. I sincerely appreciate his help on both my books.

I am indebted to all those who helped find photos for this book. Anyone who has to dig through old albums or collections will invariably get side-tracked on the mission, burning valuable time along the way. My heartfelt thanks go to Gail Hogan, Sheila Stokes, Harriet and Maggie Upton, Cynthia McCammon, Trish and Madolyn Nasworthy, Guy Choate, H.C. Zachry, Joe Henderson and my beautiful wife, Jeri. Thanks also to those subjects who patiently allowed me to track them down for a quick photo with my trusty Canon.

Thanks to several of our Adobe Lodge guides who were pressed into serving as models for the cover photo of this book. Left-to-right you will see Jim "Snake" Allen, Buryl Williams, Tony Kieffer, Charlie Bowers, Charles Fleming and Jerry Watts. All they got out of the deal was a free breakfast but danged if I didn't burn the bacon a bit. The eggs and biscuits were OK though.

Rebecca Farley at Company Printing here in San Angelo was mighty helpful in designing several choices for the cover of the book. No doubt about it – she is a creative artist for sure. More help on the cover came from my dear friends Dale and Kay Bates. Their input was invaluable.

Finally I must thank all my friends who have shared great stories with me over the years. Those included in this book are just the tip of the iceberg. All the rest, unfortunately, are submerged beneath the surface of my cloudy brain and have a poor chance of ever finding the light of day. Too many tales over too much time.

It might have been 30-40 years ago when I first heard many of the stories recounted here in these pages. Once I had the first draft of a tale, I would double-check my facts with the subject of the yarn. All too often, I learned that I had it only 80% accurate. That's what a failing memory will do to you. I am indebted to those who helped get the tales corrected. So all the stories herein contained are true to the best of our collective abilities.

Computers underline misspelled words. I would hate to own one that similarly highlighted exaggerations.

Such machines are currently unavailable anyway. Politicians own every last one of them and will never share that technology.

BIOGRAPHY

Skipper Duncan, a life-long West Texas rancher, was one of the first in the area to offer guided and outfitted hunts for deer and turkey back in 1985.

His newsletter, The Adobe Lodge News and World Report, was published and mailed to hunters nation-wide from 1985 to 2006. Since 2007, he writes all the material and maintains the AdobeLodge.com website which includes reports on all hunts produced by each hunting camp in the group. Current associated members, in addition to Skipper's Home Camp, are the McManus Camp, operated by Beaver McManus and the Mustang Ranch Camp, operated by Ben McCulloch.

A nationally published work by Skipper appeared in a collection entitled "Letters for Our Children", printed by U.S. News and World Report in 1996. (When first contacted by that magazine to submit a letter for possible inclusion in the book, Skipper was initially fearful they were filing suit for plagiarizing their name for his hunting camp newsletter.)

Skipper's former pastimes of running, banjo picking, calf roping and quail hunting far outnumber his current hobby list of reading (while riding a stationary bike in an air conditioned room) and occasional guitar playing. He especially enjoys watching his grandchildren compete in sports.

Skipper Duncan
P.O. Box 60127
San Angelo, TX 76906
325 374-7024

Email address skipper@adobelodge.com

Web site www.adobelodge.com

Made in the USA
Charleston, SC
29 September 2013